THE BEST OF BOB STEED

MERCER
UNIVERSITY PRESS

Endowed by
TOM WATSON BROWN
and
THE WATSON-BROWN FOUNDATION, INC.

THE BEST OF BOB STEED

THE NOT-SO-SERIOUS BUT SERIOUSLY ACCOMPLISHED LIFE OF ROBERT L. STEED

ROBERT L. STEED WITH CHUCK PERRY

MERCER UNIVERSITY PRESS
MACON, GEORGIA

MUP/ H894

Published by
Mercer University Press
1400 Coleman Avenue
Macon, Georgia 31207

First Edition

9 8 7 6 5 4 3 2 1

Books published by Mercer University Press are printed on acid-free paper that meets the requirements of the American National Standard for Information Sciences—Permanence of Paper for Printed Library Materials.

Book design by Burt&Burt

Library of Congress Cataloging-in-Publication Data

Steed, Robert L., 1936
[Essays. Selections]
The best of Bob Steed: the not-so-serious but seriously accomplished life of Robert L. Steed / Robert L. Steed With Chuck Perry.—First edition.
pages cm
ISBN 978-0-88146-509-9 (hardback: alk. paper)
ISBN 0-88146-509-7 (hardback: alk. paper)
1. Steed, Robert L., 1936- 2. Lawyers—Humor.
3. Law—Humor. I. Perry, Chuck. II. Title.
PN6231.L4S73 2014
818'.6020803554—dc23
2014035260

"LIFE OF BOB STEED"

A Man for All Seasons 3
From Roots to Full Bloom 9
Success at Home and Away 27
Mercer-ful Deeds and Honors 45
Half Lawyer, Half Wit 63

THE WRITINGS OF BOB STEED

WILLARD LIVES!

Moonbeam vs. the Krystal 79
A Dedicated Profession 81
Another Gay Program 83
Willard Makes the Team 86

YOUNGER LAWYERS SECTION NEWSLETTER

It's a Family Tradition 89
Is That Really His Name? 90
Who Shaved the Chihuahua? 91
Never Talk Back to a Witch Doctor 93

ESSAYS

But Doctor, Have You Hugged Your Lawyer Today? 97
And the Greedy Shall Inherit the Airwaves 103
Ladies, Leave Your Raincoats at Home;. 108
Mercer Is a Party School Now
You've Nothing to Lose But Serving Suggestions. 111
Democracy on the Run 114
Explicit Dr. Ruth Just Can't Compare to Bob and Sally 117

Daily Check of the Obituary Page Spurs a Trip Down Television's Memory Lane . . . 120
Teen-age Argot Will Bring the Decline and Fall of Our Noble Language . . . 123
Better to Shout than to Shoot . . . 125
A New Gender Gap: One Man's Tale on Chili Night . . . 127
The Ultimate Offense: A Book-selling Ploy . . . 130
Just What Does "Hammacher Schlemmer" Mean in German? . . . 133
Obese Abuse (or, Fat People Need Love Too) . . . 136
Beware of Those Jockey Shorts . . . 139
Cable TV Lets the Vandals in the Living Room . . . 141
Has Progress Come to Alabama? Ask the Fellow with a Phone in His Grave . . . 144
If Joggers Need Heavier Hands, Why Don't They Carry Bricks? . . . 146
Judge Wapner: The People's Justice . . . 149
Beware of Wives Bearing Gifts . . . 152
Blunder in Bermuda Matches Bush's Gaffe . . . 156
The "City Too Busy to Hate" Sure Ain't Too Proud to Brag . . . 159
When a Wristwatch Costs $3,192, You Can Bet It's No Bum's Ticker . . . 161
I Was about to Go Batty, but a New Cause Saved Me . . . 164
From All the Gang at Hallmark . . . 167
For Golfers, Just Trying to Decode "The Secret" Is Par for the Course . . . 170
A Ribiting Look at a Toadally Absurd Phenomenon in England . . . 173
Will an "Operation Desert Storm" Be Needed to Halt Swiss Conquest of the World? . . . 176
Chatty Chastain Audiences Need Some Gag Rules . . . 178
Learning the Ins and Outs of the High-Fashion World . . . 181
Getting a Musical Earful: Because Like, Man, That's What Rock 'n' Roll Is All About . . . 184
Purple Prince Can't Match Music Monarchs of the Past . . . 187
Where Do They Dredge Up Those Folks Who Appear in Infomercial Audiences? . . . 190

Business Types Need to Give Up on the Thought of Dressing Down 193
Women May Dress to the Nines, but Give Them Zero for Footwear 195
The Perils of Custom-tailored Genes 198
Sale of Used Rolex Watches Poses a Threat to Societal Order 200
Ban Those TV Flippers 203
Yes, It's Me and I'm in Love Again 206
State Politicians Deserve to Be Flushed with Victory 209
No Fool Like an Old Fool 211
Killing Bambi: Why Not Let the Deer Have Guns? 214
A Few Tips for Stand-up Comedians Who Don't Always Leave 'em Laughing 217
Sexists, Please Note: Women's Obsession with Hair Matched Only by Men's 219
There's Something Fishy about Those Sushi Bars 222

FOR EMILY, WHO UNDERSTANDS.

—C. PERRY

“LIFE OF BOB STEED”

A MAN FOR ALL SEASONS

The Walter F. George School of Law building at Mercer University is, by any measure, an imposing edifice. Built in 1955 by the Insurance Company of North America (INA), the three-story red brick building with white Corinthian columns, a steeple, and a bell tower exemplifies the Georgian style of architecture. If it looks strikingly familiar, that is because it was modeled after Independence Hall in Philadelphia, where INA was founded in 1792. Its location atop Coleman Hill overlooking downtown Macon, Georgia, only adds to the structure's gravitas.

By the mid-1970s, it was obvious that the Mercer School of Law had outgrown its cramped quarters in the old Harley Langdale building on campus. Seeking an alternative, a group of alumni and friends of Mercer obtained an option to purchase the abandoned Sears Roebuck building in downtown Macon, but that location failed to garner widespread support. Shortly afterward, word leaked out that the INA building might become available, but the estimated sale price of three to four million dollars was beyond Mercer's means at the time. Lamar Plunkett, influential statesman and entrepreneur who became Mercer's greatest benefactor, suggested to fellow Board of Trustees member Robert L. Steed that he look into the possibility of INA giving a portion of the sale price to Mercer in exchange for the concomitant tax benefits.

Steed, a bond attorney at Atlanta's prestigious King & Spalding law firm, soon structured a deal whereby Mercer paid

INA slightly more than one million dollars and received the balance as a gift—the largest gift in Mercer's history at the time. "We would not have the INA building without Bob Steed," said R. Kirby Godsey, Mercer's longest-serving president (1979–2006). "His creative thinking made that deal work. If you were starting from scratch trying to construct a prototypical law building, you couldn't find a better structure or location than the one we have." The new law school building was dedicated on May 4, 1979; Warren Burger, chief justice of the United States Supreme Court, was the featured speaker.

Walter F. George School of Law Building

Thirty-four years after that dedication, Bob Steed was back in the marble-clad entrance to the Walter F. George School of Law at Mercer University for another dedication. Dignitaries, friends, and alumni of Mercer milled about the lobby, most stopping to admire a newly cast bronze bust of a round-faced man wearing oversized eyeglasses. A thicket of hair crowned the large head, and a wry smile creased the corners of the mouth. The bust, brilliantly executed by famed sculptor/painter Ross R. Rossin, captured the intelligence, compassion, and wit of its subject, who stood across the room greeting well-wishers. This event, and the unveiling of the bronze bust, was held to dedicate the lobby of the Mercer School of Law to Robert L. Steed, a double Mercer graduate who served six terms on the Board of Trustees, including one as Board Chair, and who had first entered Mercer more than half a century earlier to be near his girlfriend. The Board of Trustee's resolution honoring Steed read, in part,

> Whereas Mr. Steed has received virtually every honor that can be bestowed on an individual by Mercer University, including the Outstanding Alumnus Award from the Mercer Law School,

Kirby Godsey, Bob Steed, and President William Underwood at the Bust Ceremony

> an honorary Doctor of Laws, and, in 2008 (Dec. 4), election as only the seventh Life Trustee in the history of the University;
>
> Now, therefore, be it resolved in recognition of Robert L. Steed's lifetime of meaningful service to Mercer University, that the Board of Trustees hereby designates the lobby of the Walter F. George School of Law Building as the "Robert L. Steed Lobby," in perpetual tribute to one of the institution's most loyal alumni and devoted Board members.

So much for the facts. The back story that followed from former President Godsey was far more entertaining and, ultimately, more informative:

> The interwoven history of Bob Steed and Mercer University has made Mercer a better place and made Bob Steed a better person. And Bob Steed needed to be a better person.
>
> Bob came to Mercer and made it his mission to break all the rules, to belittle all the traditions, and to challenge every decision made by the administration. I am confident that Bob made President [George B.] Connell's life miserable. He poked fun at the Baptists and often offended friends of the University with his irreverence and disrespect. It was tough to educate this young renegade. In fact, it was so tough that when he came out

of the Mercer Learning Machine the first time, he still had a few spots. So we put him through the wringer again, and this time he came out as a lawyer. The University issued a blanket apology to the profession, but his partners at King & Spalding confirmed that he was not lawyer enough to hurt. When he went to King & Spalding, their challenge was where they could put Bob so that he would do the least harm. So they stashed him away in the catacombs of the Bond Department. After all, bonds are esoteric and opaque, and bond lawyers generate tons of paper that no one reads and they charge outrageous fees that no one can justify.

Thinking Bob was safely tucked away in an obscure suburb of the law, the world could now rest easy. But it turns out that the world could not rest easy. He started writing occasional columns of humor for *The Atlanta Constitution* and then writing books, some of which, I regret to say, actually bore the imprimatur of the Mercer University Press. In the process, Bob managed to embarrass his colleagues at King & Spalding, to insult every citizen of Cobb County, and mercilessly to ridicule his lovely wife, Lu. Furthermore, he created a firestorm among Baptists, at least among those who could read. And frankly, as President of Mercer, I did not need any help when it came to making the Baptists mad.

Bob's books became legendary for their absence of intellectual value. To say the least, they are more than slightly south of Pulitzer Prize writing literature. A few titles include:

- *Willard Lives!*
- *Lucid Intervals* (in which there are none)
- *Money, Power and Sex—A Self-help Guide for All Ages*
- *Mail Fraud* (which was a fraudulent piece of work)
- *A Ship without an Udder* (based on a malapropism to which Lu is inclined).

Now, if you are utterly devoid of anything useful to read and want to see one of these books and can't find one, don't worry. Call Emily Myers [then Senior Vice President for University Advancement and External Affairs]. She probably has two or three boxes of them left in the trunk of her car. She used to give them away to donors we had given up on.

In spite of his irreverent humor and his obscure practice of law, Bob grew up to be a Trustee of the University. It was a bit of a challenge getting Bob on the Board. His wife, Lu, had surreptitiously installed him as a member of the Methodist Church, so the Baptists balked at his nomination. They were convinced that the Methodists were just intermittent churchgoers who went mostly to expunge their guilt for drinking too much. So the Methodists believed Steed was a Baptist and the Baptists hoped that he was a Methodist.

But miracles abound. This young boy from Bowdon, Georgia, despite all his irreverence and foolishness, grew up to become one of Mercer's most important Trustees and a historic Chair of the Board. When not serving as Chairman of the Board, he was Chair of the Development Committee, which turned out to be the report highlight of most meetings. He conceived the idea of the Mercer Authors Luncheon, an annual Atlanta literary event to support the University Press, and served as its master of ceremonies for more than twenty years. And I had the pleasure of appointing him to serve as an inaugural trustee of the Woodruff Trust, which supports Mercer's School of Law.

In truth, no one has ever served the University with more grace and distinction than Bob Steed. Underneath all of the nonsense and banter that Bob and I have exchanged over the years, of which I have always been on the short end, Bob Steed has made such a powerful difference at Mercer because he combines an extraordinary intelligence with an extraordinary sense of humor. In the first place, you have to be brilliant to come up with all of this nonsense. But, more importantly, his bright, quick, insightful mind always enabled us to navigate choppy waters with greater wisdom and better judgment. Over and over again, his intelligence helped us solve problems and win friends, and to keep us on track for becoming a great university. This rare combination of intelligence and linguistic genius made Bob Steed not only a lifetime but a legendary Trustee.

I close with a personal word. In my twenty-seven years at the helm of Mercer, I never knew a more loyal advocate for Mercer or any person more committed to Mercer's good future. Bob brought a keen mind, a gentle spirit, a stress-relieving sense of humor, along with a capacity for rigorous analysis to all our work together. So, I am happy to be among you to salute

> my friend and colleague, Bob Steed, as a first citizen of the Mercer Community. His wisdom, his counsel, his voice of civility, his thoughtful caring and his generous friendship made me a better President and made Mercer a better University.[1]

The journey from rural Bowdon, Georgia, to a bronze bust in the hallowed halls of Mercer University seems almost inevitable, in retrospect, as easily traversed as the hundred miles separating the two towns. But it was a journey that began not on red dirt roads but rather in a playground sandbox.

1 Text provided by Mercer University.

FROM ROOTS TO FULL BLOOM

Mercer's Robert L. Steed, like all those of his generation, was shaped by the hardscrabble, secondhand legacy of the Great Depression. His father, Robert Pentecost Steed, was born in Carrollton, Georgia, in 1912, the oldest of five children. When he was only twelve years old, Bob the elder's father, Lee Steed, died from a ruptured appendix, leaving him the *de facto* man of the house and his mother, Nona Pentecost, to provide for the family on her schoolteacher's salary. When he was old enough for high school, Robert went to stay with his cousin Velma McElroy in Rome, Georgia; Velma was the personal secretary to Martha Berry, the famous educator and founder of the boys' and girls' high schools that became a junior college in 1926 and then the four-year Berry College in 1930. Students at the high schools were required to earn their tuition by working on the school farm. Martha Berry's personal motto, and subsequently the motto of the school, was, "Not to be ministered unto but to minister." Robert (always called "Bob" by his family and friends) later regaled his sons with stories about how he drove the trash wagon and milked dozens of cows every day to earn his keep.

More of the same followed young Bob when he returned to Carrollton two years later to attend Georgia's 4th District A&M School. In 1906, the Georgia General Assembly had created an agricultural and mechanical school in each of the state's eleven congressional districts to prepare rural youth for farm life. The

Young Robert P. Steed

Young Dot Roop

4th District school's motto was, "We learn to do by doing," so students literally worked hard on their educations. Bob swept the courthouse and the local poolroom for extra money, and occasionally he slept in unoccupied jail cells rather than in his crowded home.

Being the son of a teacher, Bob valued education and tried to earn his college tuition by playing football, first at Gordon College in Barnesville (earlier Georgia Industrial College) and then at Oglethorpe University in Atlanta. At five feet eight inches and maybe one hundred fifty pounds, Bob used intensity and ferocity to hold his own with much larger players. That same fighting spirit had made him an accomplished boxer in amateur circles, so after a couple of years in college, he went to Tampa, Florida, where he aspired to be a professional boxer. As his son Michael Parker Steed recounted years later, "Dad got the crap beat out of him in Florida and astutely decided that he had to find another line of work."

That pursuit of employment led him to Bowdon, Georgia, where in 1933 Warren Sewell, who along with brothers Roy and Robert owned and operated Sewell Manufacturing, had opened a branch of their clothing factory not far from their ancestral home in Randolph County, Alabama. The Bowdon plant specialized in men's suit jackets, and Bob Steed landed a job as a "sleeve girl," so called because most of the people who did the work were women. But setting sleeves was the most difficult part of the manufacturing process and paid the highest wages, so Bob jumped at the opportunity; he earned twelve dollars per week for his efforts.

With a little money in his pocket and a little time on his hands, Bob soon met young Doris (Dot) Glen Roop of Bowdon and began a whirlwind courtship. When word got out that they were seeing each other, Dot's parents were not keen on the idea. It seems that Bob had bounced a check at the local café, and even though he soon covered the check, word of the "scandal" had spread around town. Dot's father, Q. P. Roop (named for Quanah Parker, the famous Comanche chief), was a man of few words, but his glares could stop a man in his tracks. So rather than ask permission, Bob and Dot decided to take their chances with forgiveness: they eloped to Heflin, Alabama, on June 4, 1934. That night, and for a week or so afterward, husband and wife returned to their respective homes without telling anyone of their marriage. Soon enough, Dot confessed to her mother, Winnie, who helped break the news to Q. P. The fact that the new husband had a job was said to ease the blow.

In the early-1930s, Sewell Manufacturing had begun opening company stores across the country to sell their surplus clothing. One of the stores in Washington State was not doing well, so Warren Sewell asked Bob Steed to go there and take over. The excitement of traveling cross-country and being promoted from "sleeve girl" to salesman was appealing to Bob, who accepted the offer, but after a year away, he and his young bride were homesick. Bob asked Mr. Sewell about a job opening closer to home. In fact, by the mid-1930s, Sewell had decided to get out of the retail business and had begun offering store managers the chance to buy their stores; the retail location in Augusta, Georgia, had come available. With encouragement from Mr. Sewell, Bob and Dot moved to Augusta in 1936 and opened Steed Clothing Company on Broad Street, selling Sewell-manufactured suits and hats.

Business was slow as the country eased inch by inch from the grip of the Depression, but life went on for Bob and Dot. And

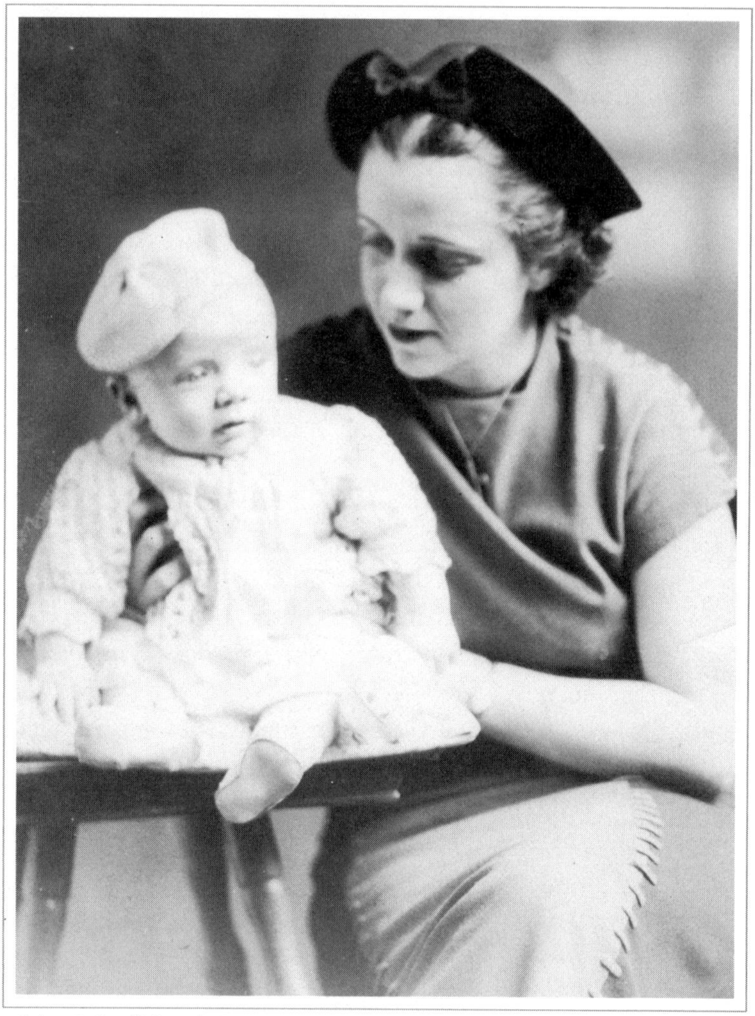

Robert L. Steed's first photo op

thus it was in Augusta, Georgia, on November 20, 1936, that Robert Lee Steed was born.

The proud parents took their new son to Bowdon to show him off to family and friends. One of Dot's friends, Mildred McElroy, also had a new child, a daughter named Linda. The friends photographed their infant babies playing together in a sandbox; the handwritten caption on the back of the photo read,

Bobby Steed served as a model for this Penney's ad in Savannah.

Brother Mike joins the Steed family in 1944.

"Bob's first playmate, Linda McElroy. Age 2 months." That was the beginning of a storybook romance.

Meanwhile, back in Augusta, the clothing business continued to drag along. After two disappointing years, Bob Steed closed his business and moved his family to Savannah, Georgia, working first for J.C. Penney and then for Sears Roebuck, where he became a merchandise manager. Dot worked in a retail dress shop, Bobby attended schools in Savannah, and on March 13, 1944, he got a brother—Michael Parker Steed. After two years, Sears transferred Bob to Jacksonville as regional merchandise manager, but that job still did not provide the stimulation he sought. "Dad was always a bit impatient," says Mike Steed. So, after another couple of years, the family packed up and moved again, this time back to Bowdon, where Bob worked as a manufacturer's rep for Botany Woolen Mills.

Twelve-year-old Bobby Steed, having grown up in cities considerably larger than Bowdon, made quite an impression when he hit town. One of those who noticed was his old sandbox playmate, Linda Ruth McElroy (Lu). "I remember being very aware of

A beanie was sophisticated in Bowdon.

Bob and Lu in the eighth grade.

this strange new boy in town," she recalls. "He dressed differently from any of the boys in Bowdon—the locals wore dungarees and T-shirts and usually went barefoot, but Bob wore corduroy pants with plaid shirts and shoes. He seemed very sophisticated. We had our first actual encounter when school started. It was in geography class, and I was locating Aswan Dam on a map. Bob came up to me and said, 'You shouldn't use words like that in public.' I was totally flustered." Bob says of Lu, "She stood out from the very start. She was distinctive. Aloof…or brain damaged. I could never tell which."[2]

Teenage dating in Bowdon in the late 1940s amounted to meeting at the local drugstore fountain for Cokes, having your mother drive you to a friend's house for a Rook party (the card game), or surreptitiously pairing up at the local movie theater on Saturday afternoons. Bobby Steed's first move on Linda McElroy was to suggest that they trade comic books. Then he started walking her around the block after Rook parties. "He tried to kiss

2 All quotations from individuals were taken from personal interviews with the author, Chuck Perry.

me once, but I told him my mother was a devout Methodist and had warned me, 'Whatever you do, don't let a boy kiss you!'" she says. "I don't know what attracted him to me, because in the eighth grade I didn't even shave my legs yet; mother was very strict about such things." Bob interjects dryly, "She looked like a tarantula." Her long, lean legs also led to an indelible nickname: "One of Bob's friends said I walked like I was planting corn, so he called me 'Loping Lulu.' Lu stuck and I've been called that ever since."

They were a twosome during their ninth grade year, always together at school, church, parties, and movies. But then, just before the start of tenth grade, Big Bob dropped another bombshell: the family was moving to Edinburg, Texas, ten miles from the Mexican border. A friend had recommended him for a store manager's position with the Terry Farris Company, a chain of department stores based in McAllen, Texas, and he had accepted the offer. "I was devastated," says Lu, "but my mother was delighted. She was afraid we were getting too close and might even be kissing, God forbid."

Texas proved to be enriching for teenage Bob Steed: he started playing football for the local high school, learned Spanish, explored parts of Mexico, attended bullfights, worked weekends in his father's store, and started driving (the legal age in Texas was fourteen, compared to sixteen in Georgia). But the Texas experience lasted only one year. Terry Farris sent a merchandise manager to the Edinburg store, and he and Bob Steed clashed from the get-go. The young man from the home office was a bit too forceful in telling Bob how to set up his store, so the veteran entrepreneur physically threw him out on the street. The home office responded by firing Steed as store manager. The Steeds returned to Bowdon and lived upstairs in

Young Bob as a Texan

The King of Cool and his infamous Packard

the Roops' house, and Bob the elder took a job as a salesman with Carrollton, Georgia-based Testworth Laboratories. The company made latex carpet backing, so he spent a lot of time working around the burgeoning carpet manufacturing industry of North Georgia.

If Bobby Steed had seemed sophisticated when he arrived in Bowdon wearing corduroy pants, he seemed absolutely alien when he returned for eleventh grade speaking a little Spanish and driving a 1949 Packard Eight. "All the girls loved Bob because he was a smooth talker and so much smarter than most Bowdon boys," says Lu. "And the fact that he was the only person in our age group with a car made him that much more popular. He started driving all our friends around town; we quadruple-dated everywhere we went, because my mother wouldn't allow me to be alone in the car with him. It was so strange: Bob's family had a couple of horses, and on Saturdays he would bring them saddled up to my house. We would ride off on horseback for the day, free as a bird with no chaperone. But if we went anywhere in the car, my mother had to know exactly where we were going, what we would be doing, who would be there, and when I would be home."

Dating on horseback...and unchaperoned

Bob the Elder was also settling into Bowdon. In 1955, at the encouragement of his friend and apparel manufacturing executive Lamar Plunkett, he began working for a manufacturer's agency selling buttons, thread, and labels in Georgia, Alabama, Florida, and Tennessee. He could live in Bowdon and learn the "findings" business, supplying apparel manufacturers in the Southeast. No doubt, the Jones Y. Pharr Company got Steed's attention by offering a company car; he tested that policy by wrecking two identical 1955 Buick Specials in one year.

In March 1957, Bob the Elder made his final career move. Again at the encouragement of his friend Lamar Plunkett, he left the security of the company-car job to start his own sales agency, which he called Steed Sales Company. With a briefcase full of samples of buttons, threads, labels, piecework tickets, and interlinings, and an office that consisted of a portable typewriter and a metal file box, he struck out building a business that would ultimately endure for fifty years, until 2007. Not surprisingly, the early years were tough; he worked hard for five years before seeing a reasonable profit for his effort. His wife, Dot, operated a ladies dress shop called the Hi-Lo Shop in partnership with her aunt. That enterprise allowed Bob the opportunity to help with merchandising, a skill from his past, while providing income to keep the family going in those early years of the sales company.

The Bowdon Steeds in 1990: (left to right) Mike, Dot, Big Bob, and Bob

Bob and Dot's younger son, Mike, came into the sales agency business after graduating from the University of Georgia in 1966. What was supposed to be a temporary job for Mike lasted more than forty years. During his time there, the company grew in personnel, sales, and profitability and also became a manufacturer of the products it sold until the majority of its customers began manufacturing and sourcing off shore. Founder Bob Steed stayed active in the company until shortly before his death in 1992. Mike has been fond of saying, "In the next incarnation, Bob will stay in Bowdon and run the family business and I will be the rich Atlanta lawyer."

* * * * *

By the end of eleventh grade, Bob and Lu were inseparable. "He told me that year that he was going to marry me," recalls Lu. "He was class president and captain of the football team, but I thought he was out of his mind. I knew I was going to college and nothing would have stopped me. My father, Lynn McElroy, was the only one in our family to finish college, and that was a big goal for me. They had already picked out Wesleyan in Macon by the time I was in ninth grade, because it was an all-girls Methodist school. Bob's family wanted him to go to an Eastern school, and they already had catalogs and applications for him. I think they were also a little wary of me and were happy for us to be apart. My folks were so eccentric and not very sociable like Bob's. My mother operated her own hair salon, didn't play bridge or go to the Blue Stocking Club." But when Lu committed to attend Wesleyan, Bob applied to Mercer because it was only a few miles away. "I didn't know anyone who had gone to Mercer, but it was a Baptist school not

Bob Steed, captain of the football team

Lu working at her mother's hair salon, Moderne Beauty.

far from home and very close to Wesleyan, so that was good enough for me," says Bob. Years later he described Mercer as a school for those "too poor to go to Emory and too proud to go to Georgia."

Wesleyan didn't make it easy for a young man with courting on his mind. "We were basically chaperoned for the first two years of college," recalls Lu. "We had supervised sign out and sign in, we always had to double-date, and freshmen and sophomores were limited to a certain number of dates per week. My mother was very pleased."

Mercer and Wesleyan were strong liberal arts schools, so Bob and Lu learned skills that would be put to good use in their futures—writing and art. As an undergraduate English major, Bob developed strong writing skills that led his fraternity brothers to nominate him as editor of the college newspaper, the Mercer *Cluster*, and he won. While in that position, he developed a humor column written under the pseudonym of Willard Clutchmyer. This mysterious character, who in drawings bore an uncanny resemblance to *Mad* magazine's Alfred E. Neuman, wrote about the humorous sides of college life, harpooning such subjects as compulsory chapel, the quality of dining hall food, and the poverty-stricken faculty. Those barbed columns kept Clutchmyer on the Mercer Ministerial Association's prayer list for as long as it was published.

Campaign card for editor of the Cluster

Bob was active as a Mercer undergraduate. He was a member of Blue Key and the Student Government Association, president of the sophomore class, and president of his fraternity, Phi Delta Theta. As fraternity president, one of Bob's roles was booking bands for weekend dance parties. "When we went off to college," says Lu Steed, "the only dances we knew were 'Glow Worm' and square dancing. Of course, no dancing was allowed on campus at either Mercer or Wesleyan, but there were dance parties almost

Bob and Lu (center) at a Phi Delta Theta house party on St. Simons Island, 1957

every weekend off campus. Before long we were doing the shag, the bop, the stroll, and all sorts of dances."

Macon was a musical hotbed of Southern rock and R&B in the late 1950s and early 1960s, and it was not unusual for Mercer students of that era to have the opportunity to see nationally renowned performers like Fats Domino, Little Richard, Otis Redding (who previously had worked with Little Richard's back-up band), Percy Sledge, and Sam and Dave. In fact, one of Otis Redding's first solo shows was at the Mercer Phi Delta Theta lodge in the early 1960s. He was booked by Phil Walden, a Phi Delt brother from Macon who had been recruited by Bob Steed. Walden and Redding became close friends, and Walden served as Otis's manager from 1959 until Redding's death in 1967. In a bit of fascinating rock music trivia, Redding was under contract with Stax records in the early 1960s, but Walden wanted to break that contract and sign him to a different label. He turned to his former fraternity brother, Bob Steed, for legal help. Steed, a young lawyer with King & Spalding in Atlanta, negotiated the deal for a $50 fee. Walden went on to become the co-founder of Capricorn Records, where he helped create the Southern rock genre and recorded such historic acts as the Allman Brothers, the Marshall Tucker Band, Elvin Bishop, Wet Willie, Bonnie Bramlett, Grinderswitch, and the Dixie Dregs.

Phil Walden and Bob Steed, friends and music lovers

Mary Travers and Steed in New York

Steed and Walden remained close friends for life (Walden died in 2006, and Bob spoke at his funeral service), and that friendship provided Bob and Lu with access to endless concerts and performers. Music became a big part of their lives and led to a close friendship with Mary Travers, the melodious blonde member of Peter, Paul and Mary who died in 2009, among others. Lu has always painted while listening to music, and her tastes are as rich and varied as the colors on her palette. From Keb Mo to Frank Sinatra and Cowboy Troy to Grace Potter, she finds soothing accompaniment for her work. In the mid-1980s, she began sharing her musical discoveries with friends at Christmas, first as a cassette tape and later as a CD. Those on her Christmas gift list look forward to her offering every year. Bob's beloved brother Mike developed the musical gene one step further—he has played guitar for the respected Bullsboro Bluegrass Band since 1973.

* * * * *

Late in their sophomore year at Mercer, Bob gave Lu his Phi Delt pin, which in those days was tantamount to being engaged. He also enrolled in Army ROTC "for the money," he says. The quid pro quo of that enlistment came upon graduation, when Bob had

Pledge fulfilled: Bob and Lu at their wedding, 1958

to report to Fort Gordon, Georgia, outside Augusta, for active military duty. The good news was that he earned $400 per month as a second lieutenant, and that was close enough to a real job for him to formally propose marriage to Linda Ruth McElroy and fulfill the pledge he had made in eleventh grade. They were married on August 23, 1958, twenty-two years after their first encounter in a sandbox.

Prior to the wedding, no one said anything about the bride and groom being fifth cousins. Mike Steed explains the genealogical separation: "You see, Lu's mother, Mildred Steed McElroy, came from the Burwell Steeds [Burwell is a community about three miles from Bowdon], who were all Methodists, while Bob came from the Roopville Steeds [Roopville is located about ten miles from Bowdon], who were all Baptists. So Bob and Lu weren't close enough kin to raise any eyebrows in rural West Central Georgia…only four miles from Alabama."

PUT THIS BOY OFF AT MACON[3]

It is difficult if not impossible to realize that the urbane, charming, well-dressed, prosperous, highly intelligent and painfully modest young attorney that all the world knows as Robert L. Steed is the same lad who only in 1954 left Bowdon, Georgia, for Mercer University after having been put on a southbound Greyhound by his mother with nothing more than a shoebox of fried chicken, two Milky Ways, forty cents in change, a rubber sheet, and a lapel sign reading "Put this boy off at Macon."

While at Mercer, Steed, a triple-threat high school footballer (run, stumble and fall), lettered on the famed Mercer squad which held a highly regarded Agnes Scott eleven to a scoreless tie for three quarters. Agnes Scott went on to win in the fourth quarter after Mercer was penalized over 600 yards for illegal use of hands.

Steed worked his way through college selling *Grit* newspapers and rolling an occasional drunk. He was also granted a small scholarship by the Baptist Student Union on the condition that he sign a pledge forswearing strong drink, movies, dancing, lustful thoughts, and intermarriage with Methodists.

He broke the last two vows in 1958 when he began courting and later married Linda McElroy, a student at Wesleyan. Miss McElroy, formerly a dancing cigarette pack on the Ted Mack Original Amateur Hour, encouraged her husband to become a profes-

3 This piece is like one of Bob Steed's "spoof biographies" (see chapter 3), except it is actually a "spoof autobiography," as he wrote it about himself.

sional man. After a brief and colorless career as a chiropodist ("I got started off on the wrong foot"), Steed became a lawyer.

Just out of law school, he was a law clerk on one of the appellate courts for over a year but quit in a fit of pique when he discovered the other law clerks were getting paid.

Steed, his wife Linda, and their small son, Cheeta, live in a reconditioned kennel in fashionable northwest Atlanta. Their home, often featured in the *Atlanta Journal*'s "Dixie Living" section, is done in a tasteful combination of several periods, the most prominent of which are Early In-Law and Goodwill Industries. (1964, excerpted from *Willard Lives!*)

A proud mother at Bob's graduation from Mercer

Reporting for duty, Sir

SUCCESS AT HOME AND AWAY

After six months of active duty in the US Army Military Police section at Fort Gordon, Georgia, Bob Steed was offered the chance to serve the remainder of his enlistment in reserve status. That freed him to enter law school at Mercer in September 1959. Law school? Where did that come from? "I don't know why I decided to become a lawyer," says Steed. "We didn't have a lawyer in Bowdon when I was growing up, and Perry Mason wasn't even a big TV star by then, but I became attracted to it while I was an undergraduate. It had several advantages over other jobs: there's no heavy lifting, most of the work is done indoors, and it pays better than selling shoes. I was also impressed by the fact that you can apparently *practice* law your whole life without ever having to master it."

Bob did well in law school, making the dean's list five times and serving as editor of the *Mercer Law Review*. He also clerked in the evenings for the century-old Macon firm of Anderson, Walker & Reichert, mostly checking titles. Lu was also being industrious: she birthed their first child, a son named Joshua Pentecost Steed, in March 1961.

Upon graduation (*cum laude*) from Mercer Law School in 1961, Bob was offered a prestigious internship with Judge Carlton Mobley, himself a graduate of Mercer Law and then a justice on the Supreme Court of Georgia. Bob committed to a two-year term with Judge Mobley but almost immediately was tempted to renege. A member of the venerable Atlanta law firm of King & Spalding, also a Mercer Law graduate, was actively recruiting young lawyers. Griffin Bell "wanted someone who was smart and had a little personality," and young Bob Steed fit the bill. "I told him about the internship with Judge Mobley but admitted I was very tempted by a real job offer from a premier Atlanta firm," recalls Steed. "Judge Bell told me to go ahead and serve the internship, that the King & Spalding job would be available afterward. And when Judge Mobley heard about my offer from King & Spalding, he agreed to reduce my internship to one year so I could take the job sooner."

Coincidentally, Bell himself was being tempted at the same time: President John F. Kennedy was about to appoint him to the Court of Appeals for the Fifth Circuit. Bell served on the Fifth Circuit until March 1976. Months later his friend Jimmy Carter was elected president and promptly nominated Judge Bell as US Attorney General, a position he held with distinction until 1979. He subsequently returned to King & Spalding, where he practiced law and counseled young lawyers until his death in January 2009. Years later, Bob Steed allegedly said to Judge Bell, "You're one of the most influential people in my life; I don't know what I'd be if I hadn't met you." Judge Bell replied, "Well, I guess I'll just have to learn to live with that."

The internship under Judge Mobley turned out brilliantly for young Steed. "It was a combination job of law clerk and secretary, but Judge Mobley was very generous and trusting and allowed me to write several opinions myself…those that he knew I was capable of handling." As planned, Bob joined King & Spalding as an associate a year later, where he was among a pool of young lawyers. "They had told me I wouldn't make less than I was

Judge Griffin Bell and his star recruit from Mercer

making under Judge Mobley, which was $750 a month. But when I told that to the managing partner, he said, 'Oh, no, that would wreck our whole salary structure. We can't pay a beginning lawyer that much!' He countered with an offer of $450 a month, and since I had already left one job and didn't have any prospects for another, I took it."

Today King & Spalding has eight hundred lawyers in seventeen offices in the United States, Europe, the Middle East, and Asia, but when Bob joined the firm in 1962, he recalls there being nineteen lawyers. "It was too small then to have distinct departments, so any lawyer could give you an assignment. We all sat in the library waiting to be picked—I didn't have a desk, a chair or an office, just yellow pads and pencils. But it was a great opportunity to experience several areas of law." Bob first worked with Byron Attridge on real estate deals, "mostly on condemnation of parcels of land. The story is told that one day I walked up to a clerk at the courthouse and she said, 'Is that a new suit?' I answered, 'No, ma'am, I've worn it since college.' After that embarrassing episode, firm lore is that I was moved to the bond department to keep me away from the public. Truth be told, it

Lawyer Bob Steed lands at King & Spalding

was more a case of Pope McIntire, the firm's bond specialist, needing a warm body to assist him on a project, so he recruited me. As haphazard as that sounds, that's exactly how my professional career was cast."

Handling the legal aspects of general obligation bonds and revenue bonds may sound dry as dust for an ambitious young lawyer with a quick wit and bristling personality, but in the context of the times, it was anything but dull. It has been argued that without the ability of state and local governments to issue debt, the United States as we know them would not exist. In 1902, outstanding state and local government debt in the US was $2.1 billion, or $27 per capita. By 1927 that amount had jumped to $14.9 billion, or $125 per capita. There followed a dramatic downturn because of the Great Depression and World War II. After the end of the war, America was faced with an extended period of drought in capital spending, a significant growth in population, and a major relocation of the population from rural to urban areas. In addition, pent-up housing demand, the changing character of transportation, and a shift in structures for manufacturing facilities all combined to produce a huge demand for additional public and private facilities. In response to that demand, the level of state and local government debt increased rapidly. At the end of 1960, the amount of outstanding state and local government debt was only $66 billion, but by the end of 1981, the amount was more than $361 billion—a 611 percent increase over twenty-one years.[4]

"Atlanta was booming in the 1960s and '70s, becoming the premier city of the New South," says Steed. "Everybody needed funding for new projects, water systems, infrastructure, and so on. Tax laws were changing rapidly, creative new debt structures were conceived; it was like the Wild West in bonds. I was going to New York four or five times a month to close deals. It was anything but dull. And Pope turned out to be a great person to work with: he was one of the smartest men I ever knew, and he gave me plenty of opportunities to step up and make a name for myself." Steed's superior intelligence equipped him to succeed in an area of law that required meticulous attention to detail and a quick grasp of new laws and alternative solutions. Judge Griffin Bell once said, "A good bond attorney must have a filing cabinet for a mind," and Steed had exactly that.

During his early years at King & Spalding, Steed also became editor of the *Younger Lawyers Section* newsletter of the Georgia/American Bar Association. The newsletter historically had been a dry compendium of goings and comings, meetings and notices. Dry writing, of course, was unacceptable to the alter ego of Willard Clutchmyer, so Steed began writing spoof biographies of the organization's officers. The newsletter suddenly became "must reading" for YLS members and even their senior partners. When Steed's term as editor of the newsletter ended, the farcical bios also ended for a couple of years. That is, until Charlie Battle became editor of the newsletter and talked Steed into coming out of retirement to write bios for new YLS members. "I take full credit for resurrecting Steed's literary career," says Battle.

4 Mayraj Fahim, Senior Fellow of the City Mayors Foundation and its local government adviser, in the article "Municipal Bonds Have Been Issued by US Local Government since 1812," originally published by City Mayors in 2005 and updated in 2007, 2009, 2010, and 2012.

"Without me, he would have been nothing more than an obscure bond attorney with an unrequited wit."

* * * * *

When Bob and Lu had first moved to Atlanta following his graduation from Mercer law school, they had rented half of a duplex apartment in East Point, not far from the state capitol and courthouses. "When Judge Mobley's wife found out where we were living," says Lu Steed, "she almost turned white. 'Why, you can't live there!' she said. 'It's not safe.' A year later when Bob went to work at King & Spalding, we got the same response: 'You live where?' They were all appalled, and no one wanted to come to our house for dinner or anything. I guess it was a little dodgy, but I loved being able to walk outside and catch the bus to Rich's downtown, which was the only place I ever went." Armed with a small down payment from Bob's grandfather, the young couple soon found a modest home near the intersection of Howell Mill Road and Interstate 75. "I remember the purchase price was $17,500," says Lu, "and it was about eleven hundred square feet. But we lived there for eleven years, and had three more children there—Georgia Glen Steed in July 1963, Nona Steed in December 1967, and Robert Lee Steed, Jr., in February 1972. I planted flowers all over the yard, painted and wall-papered the interior, and I never would have left that house if we hadn't just outgrown it."

In love with their neighborhood, Lu began the search for larger quarters for their larger family, but their preference for a modern-style home left few choices in a mostly traditional part of Atlanta. "Bob and I both wanted a modern house; we had grown up with traditional style and were just over that." She found a dead-end street not far from their neighborhood that already had a couple of modern houses; none was for sale, but there was a vacant lot available. "Of course, we didn't know how to build a modern house from scratch, and we certainly didn't know any architects, so we found a nearby house that we liked, introduced ourselves to the owners, and asked if they could recommend us to

The Steeds' first Atlanta house in wintertime garb

1968: (left to right) Nona, Georgia, and Josh Steed

Casa Steed, with plenty of wall space for artwork

their architect. We met Bob Barnett of Alan Ferry Designers for lunch one day, told him we had children, liked art and wanted space to hang it, and described the lay of the lot to him. He sketched a plan on a napkin and, with very few changes, that plan became our home from then on."

Space for art was an integral part of the new house design. But how did a young couple from Bowdon, Georgia, who had grown up with little more than family photos and mass reproductions on their walls, become such art lovers? "I was always artsy," says Lu. "Early on I leaned more toward crafts—I made my own clothes, embroidered and sewed, and I drew a little for fun. But Bob and I were both interested in art; we both took art appreciation classes in college, and in the early days we bought reproductions of famous paintings for our walls."

Lu's love of art, which soon would blossom into an impressive career as a painter, was propelled by a family tragedy. Their youngest child, Robert Lee Steed, Jr., who had been infirm since birth, died at only fifteen months old. "The following Christmas," Lu recalls, "Bob went to Rich's and bought me an easel and a box of paints for a present. I was immediately enthralled. I started reading all sorts of books on painting, one of which was Winston Churchill's *Painting as a Pastime* [1948]. I decided if he could paint for pleasure and relaxation during the war, I could certainly do it while raising three kids and grieving for another. So I began copying paintings and became a very good draftsman."

While Lu was beginning her career as an artist, Bob was indirectly supporting the careers of many Georgia artists. "I had heard that Louis Regenstein of the Atlanta law firm Kilpatrick and Cody had started a corporate art collection. I was very impressed by that and suggested that King & Spalding do the same thing; we had recently moved in to new quarters and needed lots of art for the walls, so my timing was good. I was appointed to the firm's inaugural art committee, given a budget, and charged with acquiring the best works by Georgia painters that we could find. That provided me with the opportunity to meet many of the state's best painters, as well as Lamar Dodd, the fine artist who was still head of the University of Georgia School of Art at the time. I've remained on the art committee to this day. After purchasing a painting from one woman, I commissioned her to paint a portrait of Lu, and that was like an extended painting lesson for Lu." Bob's frequent business trips to New York and the couple's love of travel worldwide provided access to many of the finest art museums in the world.

Art lovers: Steed and Lamar Dodd

Lu also sought out other teachers. "I knew at my age, with three young children, I was not going back to school, so I decided I needed a mentor. I went to the Piedmont Park Art Festival and very carefully picked out a style that I liked—realism appealed to me most—and I approached the artist, Amelia James of Atlanta, who had studied under Lamar Dodd at Georgia. She was teaching an evening art class at Callanwolde Fine Arts Center while working on her Visual Arts degree from Georgia State. So I got a double-whammy with her: I got to learn by watching her natural painting style—she is a very gifted painter—as well as hear about what she was learning in her formal arts education." Mrs. James is best known for her portraits, but she also has an enviable reputation for her sensitive paintings of flowers and gardens. "Amelia could start with a blank canvas and paint beautifully, but I'm more of a draftsman. But she gave me a great basis in realism." Today Lu Steed's portraits and still-life paintings grace many of the finest homes in Atlanta and Georgia. She is also widely known as one of the country's best painters of large commercial trucks (semis) and their drivers. Her father was a professional trucker for Standard Oil most of his work life.

* * * * *

Like Lu's father, the Steeds have always been ready to hit the road. Soon after they were married, Bob loaded his new bride into a Volkswagen Beetle and drove to her Mexico to show off the land he had fallen in love with as a high school student. "For a girl from Bowdon, Mexico in those days was wild and primitive. It was as if I had landed on the back side of the moon. We used *Sanborn's Guide* and visited every little town along the way." Dan Sanborn, a journalist from Kankakee, Illinois, moved to the Rio Grande Valley at the southern tip of Texas in the late 1940s. He opened a small travel business in McAllen, Texas, and began selling insurance to visitors going to and from Mexico (US policies were not applicable there). His *Travelog*, with mile-by-mile information, became the ultimate guide for tourists driving in Mexico. It was detailed and descriptive, almost down to the bumps on the road, including every little restau-

The VW loaded down with Mexican treasures

Bob and Lu on Acapulco Bay

rant, motel, and local convenience store. Lu still treasures her tattered copy today.

"We went to bull fights, stayed in little inns that nobody ever heard of, and ate all kinds of wonderful new food," recalls Lu. "The first time we crossed the mountains and came to the view of Acapulco Bay, I was breathless. I still get chills just thinking about it. It's one of the prettiest sights I've ever seen, and I've seen some beautiful places on this earth." In subsequent years, the Steeds and their children made more than a dozen trips to Mexico, most by car, exploring new areas and welcoming new adventures. And the indigenous art and crafts, etched into Lu's creative vision, can be seen in their Atlanta home and in her art today.

* * * * *

Lu and Bob's admiration for automobiles flows logically from their families. Lu's father, J. L. (Lynn) McElroy, drove a Standard Oil tanker for years and later owned a service station in Ranburne, Alabama, right across the state line from Bowdon. "My dad always drove nice cars—he had a Cadillac coupe and then a Chrysler Imperial," says Lu. "I always thought we were a bit superior because we had such nice cars." Bob's father, as a traveling sales rep, always needed dependable and presentable cars; he drove Packards and Buicks when given a choice. It was a hand-me-down Packard that made Bob the toast of Bowdon High School when he returned from Texas with a driver's license.

The beloved VW that took the Steeds to Mexico the first time was later replaced by a VW Bug convertible, but that was Bob and Lu's play car instead of family transportation. In 1968, Bob began to look the part of a successful lawyer by buying a one-year-old, jet-black Mercedes 250S four-door sedan with tan leather interior. He drove that prestigious model for more than a decade until it started to need more frequent attention. Bob toyed with the idea of buying a used Rolls-Royce and even test drove a couple, but that bubble was burst when Lu commented offhandedly, "You don't have enough character to drive a Rolls-Royce." With a momentarily sagging ego, Bob replaced the Benz in the Steed stable with a stately 1983 Cadillac Seville, jet black with black leather interior; the model was formally called a "slant-back," but more often it was referred to as a "bustle-butt" because of its distinctive rear. It had plenty of character.

"I really didn't realize that I had hurt his feelings," says Lu. "We were always ribbing each other. But when I found out that he was hurt, I began a secret mission to buy him a Rolls-Royce with my own money." Not just any Rolls-Royce, but a classic Rolls that oozed character. Lu's father, Lynn, heard about a retired chemist in Douglasville, Georgia, who had collected several Rolls-Royces. Lynn determined which one had the strongest engine, and Lu soon negotiated the sale; Lu owned a 1961 Rolls-Royce Silver Cloud—a massive piece of automotive sculpture, seventeen and one-half feet long and weighing more than two tons. The turning circle of this behemoth was more than forty-one feet. The interior

The Boys—Gary (left) and El Buchanon—begin restoration of the Rolls

was swathed in Connolly leather, Wilton wool, and burled walnut. And the whole thing needed restoring.

Lynn McElroy towed the Rolls to his garage in Ranburne. He would oversee the restoration done by mechanics who had worked for him since they were in high school. "The Boys," as Lu called them, were very proficient with American metal, but none of them had ever seen the insides of a sophisticated, hand-built Rolls-Royce. Undaunted, they began disassembling the Rolls, and Lu began a global, nonstop search for restoration parts. "I combed through *Hemmings Motor News* for parts," she says, "called all over the country, and ended up ordering some parts directly from England. I had bought this car without Bob's knowledge, and now I was up to my neck in a restoration project. When he found out about it, he wouldn't even go to see it. He acted like he had no interest. It was so depressing." That depression was only a prelude: Lu's father died before the eighteen-month restoration could be completed. She and The Boys soldiered on, just as they knew Lynn would want them to. At one point, when the task at hand exceeded their collective skills, Lu contacted an Atlanta Rolls-Royce repair shop, explained the situation, and asked if she could bring The Boys by for a little guidance; everybody, including the Rolls mechanics, learned something that day.

Lu's painting of Bob and his Rolls-Royce, with the backdrop of Atlanta's 191 Building, took more than a decade to complete.

When the restoration was finally completed, Lu arranged a barbecue for the unveiling. That was the first time that Bob had seen or driven the car. He, like everyone in attendance, was overwhelmed by the grand old lady, skillfully restored to her former glory. Bob has driven the Rolls regularly since accepting Lu's gift, paid for entirely by her painting money, and now everyone agrees that he has plenty of character to drive a Rolls-Royce.

* * * * *

The Steeds' loving relationship has often been evident in Bob's writings. With tongue firmly planted in his cheek, he has referred to Lu as "…101 pounds of grit, gristle and ingratitude"; "my grizzled spouse, undaunted by her advancing years"; "a dark, severe item to whom I have been contractually committed for years"; and "…my first wife." Steed has also said of Lu, "Deep down, though she covers it up very well, she's eternally grateful that I took her out of Bowdon, Georgia, and spared her from an otherwise certain life of selling scuppernongs from the back of a pickup truck or reading palms in a dingy trailer."

Bob especially makes fun of Lu's frequent malapropisms. As he is fond of saying, "English is her second language. We haven't discovered her first yet." Among her most popular malapropisms are "You can kiss that out the window" and "It happened in one clean swoop." Lu responds, "I treat conversation and everything else just like painting, like trial and error. The fact that I don't do conversation well has never deterred me."

Here is Bob's take on her special talent:

MY WIFE, SHE'S AS FUNNY AS CROESUS

Perhaps one of the most anxious moments in modern times is the lapse between asking an old friend whom you have not seen for some time the question, "How's your wife?", and getting the answer, "Compared to what?"

I ask the question almost by reflex and then mentally bite my knuckle and worry that he's going to pull a face, look down at his shoes and say: (1) "We've been divorced for three years"; (2) "She went back to law school and filed her own divorce"; or (3) "I'm living with my dental hygienist."

I bring this up because someone mentioned to me the other day that he was reluctant to ask after my sinewy spouse because I hadn't written anything about her in many months. I was happy to report to him that the union has not yet been put asunder. It continues to be, as Jimmy Durante used to say in describing his band leader's job, "hanging by a tread."

My friend looked a little dubious and suggested that if she didn't surface soon in my literary endeavors, he might send the authorities around to dig up my patio.

Actually, we should be separated. I should be living in our home and she should be in the Intensive Care Wing of the State Home for the Verbally Dyslexic in Valdosta. However, I wouldn't dream of splitting up. Aside from the fact that during a distant fit of passion I put the house in her name, I'm also hooked for the long haul because I simply can't wait to hear what bizarre utterance she will come up with next.

I have publicly affirmed in previous essays that her curiously colorful but unconventional speech patterns result not from a lack of brain power—she is as smart as any ninety-pound person I know—but rather a monumentally bad ear.

Her mangling of our mother tongue takes many forms. Sometimes, all of the words are right but the sentiment sought to be expressed is as fuzzy as a cheap sweater. Speaking of a friend of ours, she proclaimed, "Cynthia is so much like herself, she doesn't even know it." If one is not listening carefully, such an observation will appear to make sense. However, if it actually registers in the conscious level and is analyzed, it will cause blurred vision and a ringing sensation in one's ears.

She recently told our friend Allison that, "Nothing goes past me with you." He struggled for a moment trying to glean the essence of that offering but ultimately his eyes glazed over like a sugar doughnut and his lips began to move wordlessly.

Others are just about fifteen degrees off: "He would leave no leaf unturned"; "That fellow is very unsophisticated; he seems almost like a clout"; "I don't squelch on my bets"; "Byron likes to sit around and pontiferate"; "It's a mute question."

No cliché is safe from her maladroit touch. In the space of three days she said something was "hot as Croesus," later described a house as having been "dark as Croesus," and told someone a day later that a town was "as far as Croesus." Croesus never imagined that his riches could be counted in similes.

Sometimes her utterings sound as though they carry with them an undercurrent of folk wisdom but, on analysis, simply slither into the surreal. We went to a commercial art gallery recently and the director came up and mildly remonstrated with us for not having been by for some time. My wife established good eye contact with the poor woman and said, "He moves the best who yanks the hardest." The gallery owner slumped visibly, her brow furrowed and one eye seemed to drift toward her nose. I'm sure she thought she had just suffered a small stroke.

Frankly, I don't think even the folks in Valdosta would be equal to the challenge. But, on the other hand, as our daughter once speculated after her mother had uttered a particularly mind-bruising malapropism, "Wouldn't it be funny if when she got old and senile everything started coming out right?"

Indeed; as funny as Croesus. (December 1987)

MERCER-FUL DEEDS AND HONORS

On December 4, 2008, Mercer University's Board of Trustees selected Robert L. Steed as only the seventh Life Trustee in the history of the university, following a formal nomination by Mercer President William D. Underwood. Bob had served as a Mercer trustee continuously since 1972, including one term as board chair (1985–1990). Over the years, this double Mercer graduate had also received the Outstanding Alumnus Award from the Mercer Law School and an honorary Doctor of Laws degree while becoming one of the country's most respected bond attorneys. In retrospect, nominating Steed to be a Mercer trustee seems like a no-brainer, but at the time Dr. Kirby Godsey made that bold proposal, Bob was "only" a successful attorney who wrote occasional humorous op-ed columns for the Atlanta newspapers.

"In an act of desperation intended to pique the Southern Baptist Convention, Mercer Press published a collection of my Willard columns [*Willard Lives!*] in 1981," says Bob. "Kirby Godsey, who had been named president of Mercer in 1979 despite the fact that he had a sense of humor, was intrigued by those columns and others that I was writing for *The Atlanta Constitution*. In an act of desperation again intended to pique the Southern Baptist Convention, which was staunchly opposed to humor in any form, Kirby nominated me as a trustee. At least, that's how I think it happened."

President William Underwood, Bob Steed, and Bob Hatcher

Bob Hatcher, Judge Griffen Bell, and Bob Steed at Mercer Trustees meeting

Mercer super-supporters Lamar Plunkett and Bob Steed

Two of Mercer's most illustrious alumni also played a role in Steed's appointment as a trustee. Lamar Plunkett, Mercer's greatest benefactor of the twentieth century, "looked after Bob as if he were a son," says Dr. Godsey. "Bob's father and Lamar had worked together in Bowdon, both were from similar backgrounds, and there was great respect between them. Lamar was eager to see Bob move up in Mercer circles and supported his nomination." Judge Griffin Bell, who had first offered Steed a job at King & Spalding, also supported Bob. "I believe Bob was the primary reason that Griffin Bell was so deeply involved in Mercer," Dr. Godsey continues. "Judge Bell's devotion to Mercer was matched only by his devotion to Bob; he loved him dearly. Bob was closer to Griffin than anyone in the firm, and he assured that Judge Bell never lost interest in Mercer. If Mercer was going through something difficult, Bob was the interpreter for Judge Bell, the one who explained to him what was going on. He played a crucial role in maintaining that great relationship."

Judge Bell regaled the audience with humorous recollections on the occasion of Steed's being named a Life Trustee. "I was managing partner at King & Spalding several times, and every time I had trouble with Bob. He wrote a newspaper column—he posed as a journalist. He had long since left the trial practice after about a year and he became a bond lawyer, which we trial lawyers put in the category of a 'loan closer.' So, that's what he was doing, ostensibly, for a living—and posing as a journalist, hanging out with journalists at all times (it seemed to me). And we gradually lost business on account of him.

Judge Griffin Bell, Governor Carl Sanders, and Bob Steed

"He would write bad things about doctors. Finally, we didn't have any doctors left. Then he next took out after the dentists. He wrote a column entitled, 'Why Is My Dentist a Free Man?' The Dental Association sent a committee to the law firm to see if we couldn't bring him under control. And I had to say the same thing the Mercer Dean had said to me about Steed years before when I was recruiting graduates: 'We don't know what to do with him.'

"So, it was like that all along. The crowning blow probably was when he wrote a column poking fun at the Cobb County Symphony. Well, Bob didn't have any idea what was in Cobb County—at least, he didn't know they had a symphony. But he soon found out they did have a symphony...and so there went most of our Cobb County clients."

Doc Schneider, a Mercer Law graduate and partner at King & Spalding, added to the merriment. "Bob has made a career out of being in love with Mercer University. He's been an evangelist for this University, and I'm one of his products—I may not be a good one, but I'm one of the folks that just learned to love Mercer University from Bob Steed. And I think that's his greatest gift to this University.

"Bob, as everybody knows, is a great promoter of people. He attaches himself to them and makes them bigger than what they are. That's true in my case, and it's true in the case of so many others. It reminds me of Boswell and Johnson. Boswell spent all that time writing the story of Dr. Johnson—Bob is both the writer and the story! I know that it's great to be promoted by him and to talk about him as a character. He is the person to whom I credit my coming to Mercer Law School, because it was his ingenious idea to gift/purchase that shining building on a hill that made a goofball like me (who was impressed by flashy things) to say, 'Hmm, Mercer looks pretty good to me!'"

* * * * *

Bob Steed earned his stripes as chairman of the Mercer Board of Trustees. The university confronted a number of challenges during Dr. Godsey's administration, primarily due to the school's rapid expansion after his arrival in 1977 and his installation as president in April 1980. As Lamar Plunkett said in his biography, *A Gift for Giving*, "I doubt if there's a small private comprehensive university anywhere that has schools of liberal arts, law, business, education, graduate school, pharmacy, medicine, engineering, and a university press. These were Kirby Godsey's dreams, and they have become a reality."[5] Bob Steed's time as a Mercer trustee, and especially his tenure as board chairman from 1985–1990, overlapped most of that expansion.

"Bob was, without any exaggeration, one of the most important trustees the university has ever had," says Dr. Godsey. "He was a confidante to me, someone with whom I could discuss issues and options. When the Bessie Tift issue came up in 1987, I knew that was going to be a controversial situation, and the first person I went to talk to was Bob. Together we met with Lamar Plunkett and made the difficult decision to close the school. Bob and I were in the cauldron together, but I couldn't have been in that stew with anyone better. He was incredibly loyal to the

5 James C. Bryant, *A Gift for Giving: The Story of Lamar Rich Plunkett* (Macon GA: Mercer University Press, 1993).

Steed's portrait presented to Mercer president Kirby Godsey

school; he never spoke ill of anyone, even when we were under assault; and his sense of humor helped us through many tense situations. Bob could diffuse the tension in a room quicker than anyone I've ever seen."

During the late 1980s, the closing of Tift and the Atlanta campus and the rise of the medical and engineering schools created financial stress for Mercer. "One day I met with Bob in his office to alert him that we were going to have a budget deficit for the year," recalls Dr. Godsey. "As soon as I told him, a sick look came over his face. He turned pale and was squirming in his chair. I had no idea he would take it so hard. I left his office pretty disheartened, but later that day I learned that he was having an attack of kidney stones. He was in pain, all right, but not from the news I had delivered. I was greatly relieved." Despite their close relationship, Steed kept the university's interests front and center during those turbulent times. "Anytime you have a financial downturn, it's necessary to check to be sure that nothing fraudulent was going on," says Dr. Godsey. "So Bob picked the most contrary members of the Board of Trustees to investigate my handling of those situations. I gave him a hard time about it and asked, 'Couldn't you have picked just one person who was more sympathetic?' But he knew if we passed muster with that committee, everybody else would be reassured. He always did what was best for the institution."

Steed helped Mercer tackle its financial woes with the same energy he brought to every issue. He became executive vice chairman of the Mercer University Vision 2000 Campaign, which raised capital and endowment for Mercer in excess of $200 million, the most successful fundraising campaign in the school's history at that time. "That campaign led us out of a troubled time," says Dr. Godsey. "Then, as always, Bob never turned us down when we asked him to serve. He also introduced the school to people who had the capacity to give. He brought Tom Watson Brown to us, the Harvard graduate who became one of Mercer's leading benefactors and took personal pride in growing the Mercer University Press. Bob started the annual Mercer Book and Author's Luncheon, which has brought money and prestige to the Press. He attracted famous authors from Pat Conroy, Stuart Woods, and Terry Kay to our own graduate Dr. Ferrol Sams Jr. Bob introduced us to powerful and wealthy people from all over the country, including foundations like Woodruff; he shared his personal credibility with the university. And through the years, he donated all of his speaking honoraria to Mercer. I can honestly say that Mercer never had a more loyal alumnus than Bob Steed. I know he originally came to Mercer because Lu went to Wesleyan, but I'm convinced that we got the best of that deal."

Emily Myers, who served as senior vice president of University Advancement and External Affairs at Mercer University from 1979–2008, echoes Dr. Godsey's sentiments. "I've had the privilege of working with many volunteers, trustees, and donors through the years, but not one of those ever loved Mercer University more than Bob Steed. In my role as chief development officer, having someone like Bob to help with fundraising was truly a blessing. Many people are reluctant to ask for money, but Bob was undaunted. And his polished style was so natural, his humor so endearing, that most people felt good after they were asked," said Myers, whom the Mercer Board of Trustees honored in 2011 by naming the university's new admissions and welcome center in her honor.

"Two things in particular come to mind when I think of Bob," Myers adds. "One, he is the most loyal, dependable and true-to-his-word person I've ever known. Whatever he told you he would do, he did in spades, with his full energy and effort. And two, regardless of your status or station in life, he gave everyone the very best of himself. He is the eternal optimist, always believing that everyone will 'do what is right,' as he often said.

Emily Myers and Bob Steed

"If you were Bob's friend, or worked with him in any way, you were grateful for that opportunity. His grace and humor can make even the dullest meeting seem worthwhile. I'll give you a great example," says Myers. "Once, when Mercer was in the midst of a very difficult economic situation and Bob was chairman of the Board of Trustees, we had a private meeting in the Woodruff House to inform the board. It was a very hard meeting, with people demanding explanations and venting their frustrations. The only thing that stopped that meeting was a scheduled public meeting for basically the same purpose with the faculty and staff. Bob was seated on the stage of the Medical School auditorium with President Godsey and another couple of trustees. The tension in the room was so palpable that you could have cut it with a knife. If ever there were a hostile audience, this was it. As Bob got up from his chair and started for the podium, he slipped on the stage floor and did almost a full split. For a moment I was sure he was going down. The whole audience gasped in unison, and in that moment of silence, as Bob regained his footing and composure, he said without missing a beat, 'Like a pig on ice!' The entire audience erupted in laughter. And in that instance, the tension in the room was defused. It was almost as if everyone took a deep breath, calmed down, and the meeting went on to be very productive. No one but Bob could have pulled that off."

Only five years after the successful Mercer University Vision 2000 Campaign, Steed and Judge Griffin Bell co-chaired another major capital campaign. Working with Myers, the university's Advancing the Vision Campaign raised more than $350 million, the largest fundraising initiative in the school's 175-year history. "Bob was a master at working with Judge Bell to raise money for Mercer," says Myers. "Bob and I would identify potential donors, and the Judge put his reputation on the line because he knew beyond a doubt that he could trust Bob Steed."

Steed felt the same way about Myers. He referred to her as "the wind beneath my wings" during his term as chairman of the Board of Trustees. And Lu Steed, never missing an opportunity for malapropism, said, "Mercer without Emily Myers would be like a ship without an udder."

Illustration from cover of A Ship without an Udder, *by Jack Davis*

Della Wager Wells, a partner at Atlanta's prestigious Alston & Bird law firm, is another of Steed's many admirers. As a new lawyer at King & Spalding in the mid-1980s, one of her first assignments was to write a centennial history of the firm, *The First Hundred Years: A Centennial History of King & Spalding.*[6] "Bob opened doors for me that only he could have opened. He knew everybody and made it possible for me to interview anyone—from President Jimmy Carter, former Senator Herman Talmadge and former Governor Ellis Arnall to the Coca-Cola and Trust Company leadership; Bob had widespread credibility," says Wells. "When King & Spalding decided it was time to open a New York office in 1990, Judge Griffin Bell wanted to send Bob because of his ability to charm anyone."

6 Atlanta: King & Spalding, 1985.

President Jimmy Carter being interviewed by Della Wells

Steed was always willing to share his immense knowledge and insight with others. "When he discovered that I was a voracious reader like him," Wells says, "he brought me a book of stories by S. J. Perelman. It was clear that Perelman's style had influenced Bob's writing style—wry, self-deprecating, full of word play. But as funny as Bob is on paper, he is much funnier across the desk. He has an amazing mind, lightning quick and clever. And although it may not be as much fun, he is also one of the most learned Constitutional lawyers I've ever met."

Steed's humor could surface anywhere at any time. Wells recalls a meeting with the sole Towns county commissioner about a hospital bond issue. "We were sitting outside the commissioner's office, waiting to see him. Bob had recently written a column ridiculing women for wearing sneakers to work and then changing into high heels for the office. He thought it was deplorable. He looked down at my rather large feet and said, 'Take off your shoes.' I said, 'What?' He said, 'Take off your shoes. I want to see if it's really that hard to walk in high heels.' So he took off his shoes, stepped into my high heels, and was sashaying around the room when the commissioner opened his door and came out. 'Mr. Steed!' he said. Anyone else might have been embarrassed, but Bob was as cool as could be. We always had so much fun working together."

Ruth West, another Mercer Law grad and the first woman elected to King & Spalding's partnership in 1980, also has praise aplenty for Steed: "Bob is the most generous man with his time and intellect that I have ever met. All the law clerks wanted to work with him because they learned so much and he was never critical, even when he had to correct them. We were all fortunate to have him in our midst."

President William Underwood, who became Mercer's eighteenth president in 2006 when Kirby Godsey retired, is also effusive about Steed: "Bob Steed's institutional knowledge, spanning seven decades, has been invaluable to me. He, along with Judge Griffin Bell and Kirby Godsey, helped me to understand the great character of Mercer University. Bob is totally without guile; Mercer is always first and foremost in his heart, and I have always been able to rely on his wisdom and judgment."

During President Underwood's tenure so far, enrollment at Mercer has increased by more than 20 percent to more than 8,400 students. Mercer has launched second and third medical school campuses (Savannah and Columbus), initiated a master's-level physician assistant program and a doctoral-level program in physical therapy, and added PhD programs in Clinical Psychology, Nursing, Counseling, Educational Leadership, and Curriculum and Instruction. A particular focus has been on the expansion of the university's research activities.

"Bob has stood with me as we have aggressively moved Mercer to create knowledge, not just disseminate knowledge," says President Underwood. In the last six years, the number of PhD students has increased from fewer than twenty-five to more than three hundred, while the amount of externally funded research expenditures has grown to more than $30 million. "For years Mercer was a small liberal arts college with a law school attached. But throughout Kirby Godsey's presidency and continuing through mine, we have become an emerging national research university. That transformation could not have occurred without Kirby's leadership, and Kirby's leadership could not have occurred without Bob Steed's rock-solid support in the face of sometimes fierce opposition. It's fair to say that Mercer of the future wouldn't be possible without Bob Steed."

* * * * *

Service has always been second nature for Steed, whether for Mercer or other institutions. The following are some of the many other ways Robert L. Steed has served Mercer University, Atlanta, and Georgia through the years:

- State Bar of Georgia Board of Governors, 1967–1968
- President, Younger Lawyers Section of the State Bar, 1967–1968
- Mercer Alumni Association Executive Committee, 1970–1973
- Chairman, Mercer Law School Board of Visitors, 1970–1971, 1972–1973
- Mercer University Trustee, 1972–present
- Chairman, Mercer University Board of Trustees, 1985–1990
- Member of the President's Council of Mercer University, 1977–1979, 1984–1985
- Chairman, Special Gifts Committee for Renovation of the Mercer Law School Building
- Chairman, Committee to Select Mercer Law School Dean
- Mercer University Outstanding Alumnus Award, 1985
- Mercer College of Liberal Arts Distinguished Alumnus Award, 1994
- Board Member, Walter F. George Foundation for Mercer Law School, 1986
- Trustee, George Woodruff Trust for the Mercer Law School

Steed being awarded an honorary Doctor of Laws, 1979: (left to right) Judge Griffin Bell, Chief Justice Warren Burger, Steed, then Mercer President Rufus Harris

- Executive Vice Chairman, Mercer University Vision 2000 Campaign
- Member and Vice Chairman, Metropolitan Atlanta Crime Commission
- Member, Board of Sponsors, Atlanta College of Art
- University of Georgia Gridiron Secret Society
- Director, Capital City Club, 1982–1989
- Director, Georgia Chamber of Commerce, 1982–1985
- Chairman, Georgia Chamber of Commerce Red Carpet Tour, 1979–1980
- Chairman, Georgia Chamber of Commerce Industrial Development Commission, 1982–1983
- Member, Board of Directors of Business Council of Georgia, 1983–1985
- Member, American College of Bond Counsel

- Member, Board of Directors of Clifton Corridor Council (Georgia Biomedical Partnership), 1990–1995
- Member, Board of Directors of 11 Alive Community Service Awards, 1984–1996

Of course, his greatest accomplishment is his lifelong relationship with Linda "Lu" McElroy Steed. On the occasion of their thirtieth anniversary in 1988, Bob wrote his assessment of the relationship that started in a sandbox:

THIRTY YEARS ON, HERE'S TO ANOTHER FUN-FILLED THIRTY

Aug. 23, 1988, marked the thirtieth year since my sinewy spouse and I jumped the broomstick on a hot and hazy day in a tasteful double-ring ceremony in Bowdon, Georgia.

The better element in Bowdon still recalls in admiring tones the lavish reception staged by the proud parents of the bride at the Greyhound Bus Station in Carrollton, where friends and relatives gorged themselves on cheese straws and Spam canapés surrounding a punch bowl in which a large block of lime sherbet floated sluggishly in a sea of ginger ale.

The father of the bride was heard to say, "Damn the expense; these are my friends."

Notwithstanding the fact that this union, widely acknowledged to be a mismatch across social and class lines, has endured for three decades, there still are those who enthusiastically accuse me of saying and writing "rude and insensitive things" about my wiry wife.

I, of course, vigorously and vehemently deny this allegation, pointing out that I would never say anything rude or insensitive about my bride for a number of reasons. First, she's mean as a snake, vicious, cunning and cruel, and second, as any husband with a grain of sense knows, there comes a time in every twenty-four-hour day when the husband is in bed asleep while the wife is still up stalking about. If the husband has truly gotten crossways in the stream with the wife, she can

Bob and Lu: a lifelong romance

seize upon that unhappy moment to take up some blunt, or, worse yet, sharp, instrument and do him some grievous bodily harm.

There are ample reasons beyond fear that keep me from uttering rude and insensitive things about my wife. She has many admirable qualities which, looking back from the perspective of thirty years together, I recognize and esteem.

To list just a few by way of public tribute, I offer the following:

(1) She can still wear the wedding dress which she crafted with her own hands in 1958, while I would not be able to get into my dark blue wash-and-wear suit by Haspel with a large shoe horn and a can of Crisco.

(2) She still looks good in a bikini, while I was recently asked by a lifeguard to either get a top to my bathing suit or leave the beach.

(3) She is one of the most energetic housekeepers ever to polish a plant leaf. Many is the time when I have gotten up in the middle of the evening to go to the bathroom and returned to find my side of the bed made up. She has a deep urge to Windex things that borders on compulsion. She once Windexed a torpid house guest who made the mistake of staying in one spot too long. He recommended we put her on the waiting list at the Betty Ford Center for Ammonia Abuse.

(4) She is possessed of courage rare in one so slight and old. She will fly parachutes at the beach, ride hot-air balloons in foreign countries, has gone to Egypt and Africa without me and once voluntarily witnessed an autopsy. I, on the other hand, send her downstairs to investigate things that go bump in the night and was almost eighteen before I would ride anything on the Merry-Go-Round other than the bench.

(5) She is the most energetic and resourceful provider of malapropisms I have ever encountered. Recently,

Lu Steed on safari in Kenya, 1986

while discussing a portrait she was painting, she was a party to the following exchange:

SHE: "I'm going to put a flag in that painting but it's got to be 'obsteturous.'"

ME: "What do you mean by 'obsteturous'?"

SHE: "Well, obsteturous means 'in the way' so I guess I should have said 'unobsteturous.'"

I could go on but the point is that I believe every truly sensitive husband, like myself, should occasionally (at least every thirty years) count and catalog his marital blessings and, beyond that, should publicly acknowledge them. This would go a long way toward holding down the rampant divorce rate now galloping through our connubial ranks.

When asked by others about the longevity of our union, I often quote Paul Newman, another lifer in the marriage game, who, answering the same query, said, "Think of murder but never divorce."

I think of murder every time she snorts and chortles over a winning gin hand but, with luck, I hope to hang in there for at least another thirty and, in the meantime, borrowing the words of a Dick Haymes song popular in the 1940s, I publicly proclaim to the one whose heavy-lidded gaze still causes heavy breathing on my part, "I'll Get By as Long as I Have You."

Bob and Lu aboard a camel in Agadir, Morocco, circa 1988

The Steed children and grandchildren, circa 2010: (front, left to right) Parker Steed, Nona Bickers, Lee Steed, Josh Steed, Georgia Vance, Wesley Vance, Salem Vance (back, left to right) Max Bickers, Laney Steed, Steele Bickers, Beau Vance, Lynch Bickers, Eli Bickers

HALF LAWYER, HALF WIT

Bob Steed was attracted to writing from an early age, beginning with his editorship of the Bowdon High School student paper, the *Complete Angler*. He subsequently served as editor of the *Mercer Cluster*, the *Mercer Law Review*, and the Georgia Bar Association's *Younger Lawyers Section Newsletter* before becoming a "dilettante columnist," as he described his work for the Atlanta newspapers.

In a 1984 mock interview for *Atlanta Weekly Magazine*, Steed offered some insight into his lust for writing:

> *Why would a prominent, wealthy attorney also want to write?* I'm afraid you'll have to ask a prominent, wealthy attorney that one.
>
> *Why do you write?* A great philosopher once said (I think it was either St. Francis of Assisi, Arthur Schopenhauer or Merv Griffin), "The artist himself is the poorest choice to explain his art or motives for it." Having thus disqualified myself, perhaps the keenest available source for that truth is my faithful marriage companion. When asked by an awed reader as to why I devoted the time, the energy, the unremitting dedication to writing my column, she, with the unconscious insight so often found in those who live in close proximity to genius, said, "I think he knows it's an easy way to get a picture of his big fat head in the newspaper."
>
> *Former U.S. Attorney General Griffin Bell says lawyers consider you a writer and writers call you a lawyer. What's your*

Bob flanked by his mother and father at a book signing for Lucid Intervals

reaction? Judge Bell was just being kind. My other law partners call me "half lawyer, half wit."

Does your wife, who often bears the brunt of some of your jokes, have any right to censor your works? I can write anything I want as long as I don't mind eating at Arby's and sleeping in the car.

Do you secretly long to write a serious work? You obviously haven't read one of my trust indentures.

Does your writing interfere with your legal practice? It probably interferes because, although there are many, many people who encourage me to give up the law practice and take up writing full-time, it is significant that most of them are either my law partners or my clients.

Six volumes of Bob Steed's wit and wisdom have been published, and thousands of his delightful letters have been saved by their recipients. His published works include:

Willard Lives! (Mercer University Press, 1981)

Lucid Intervals (Mercer University Press, 1983)

Money, Power and Sex (A Self-Help Guide for All Ages) (Mercer University Press, 1985)

The Sass Menagerie (Longstreet Press, 1988)

Mail Fraud, The Laughable Letters of Robert L. Steed (Longstreet Press, 1988)

A Ship without an Udder (Longstreet Press, 1995)

Not surprisingly, all of the proceeds from Steed's publishing ventures have gone to Mercer. Since nothing speaks louder about the quality of his written work than the work itself, the following are samples through the years.

The spouse parade: (L-R) Josh and Robbin Steed, Burton and Georgia Vance, David and Nona Bickers, Bob and Lu Steed

A Baltic cruise with friends: (back L-R) Bob Long, Bob Steed, Bob Wells, Anne Goodsell, Judy Allison, Lu Steed, (front L-R) Jane Long, Dick Allison, Ann Klamon, Dick Goodsell, Ruth West Wells, Larry Klamon

Mercer Authors Luncheon gathering: (back, L-R) Marc Jolley, Dr. Ferrol Sams Jr., Chuck Perry, Bob Steed, (front L-R) Tom Watson Brown, Dr. Helen Sams

In the late 1980s, Mercer hosted an annual celebrity golf tournament to raise funds for the school. This classic group includes (L-R) Chi Chi Rodriguez, Calvin Peete, Bob Steed, Andy Bean, Hubert Green, and Fuzzy Zoeller.

Another year, Judge Griffin Bell and Steed hosted Jack Nicklaus.

Artist Steve Penley presents Steed with a portrait for the Casa Steed gallery.

The YKK company of Macon, the world's leading manufacturer of zippers and hook and loop closures, has been a great supporter of Mercer. As a "thank you," Bob Steed, President Kirby Godsey and Macon Mayor Buck Melton traveled to Japan in the 1990s to present a portrait to YKK founder Tadao Yoshida.

Due to Steed's quick wit, he was in great demand as a master of ceremonies. Here he talks with lawyer Gail Massee and writer Jimmy Breslin at a 1978 Atlanta Bar Association meeting...and roasts Georgia football coach Vince Dooley at a fundraiser for Juvenile Diabetes.

Steed himself was roasted by friends in a Macon fundraiser. Roasters included (L-R) Judge Griffin Bell, Macon Mayor Buck Melton and Jack Watson.

Still drawn to Mexico, the Steeds visit Cabo San Lucas twice a year. Friends on a recent trip included (front L-R) Steve and Carrie Penley, Bob and Lu Steed, Alex and Todd Holleman, (back L-R) Karen Hudson, Julia Huston.

A family breakfast at the White House Restaurant in Atlanta is a Steed-family Christmas tradition. This photo is from the 2007 celebration.

THE WRITINGS OF BOB STEED

WILLARD LIVES!

MOONBEAM VS. THE KRYSTAL

It was Wednesday night in M.E.P. and the coeds were chasing up and down the halls throwing fried chicken at each other. I had a date with Moonbeam. We were planning to go down to the auditorium to watch the city council wrestle the Ku Klux Klan in a one-hour tag-team match.

I tiptoed up to the date desk and asked the ominous looking female attendant to call my date. She swore at me for a time but finally punched the button. "Hey, Fatso," she screamed to Moonbeam through the speaker, "your idiot boyfriend is here. Wait in there," she said, pushing me into the overstuffed parlor across the hall.

The room was dimly lit but I could see Miss Yachoo Pendant, assistant professor of Mercer's Oriental Social Sciences department, huddled in the far corner. She was enjoying a light snack of dried squid and saki. Everyone knew she was the hardest teacher on the entire campi. In the sixty-one years she had been here, only one person, Oliver Nosewell, class of '09, had made an A. And to get it he had to pull her to Warner Robbins and back twice a day in a rickshaw.

As I waited for Moonbeam, another coed, Baby Doll von Voluptuous, floated by in a low-cut, I said low-cut, evening gown. I couldn't tell if she was in it and trying to get out, or out of it trying to get back in. Several other strapless girls came breezing by talking excitedly. I found out that there was gala dance that night and the girls had late permission (10:30).

While I waited, in walked Udine Cutlass, who was in a very jovial mood. "How goes it, Udine?" I asked in my most gracious manner.

"Pretty good, Willard," he countered. "We had an open-book test in history today, and I really ate it up."

"I didn't know your teacher gave open-book tests," I exclaimed.

"The professor doesn't know it either," whispered Udine, looking under all the sofas for concealed Honor Council members. "Man," he said in a hushed tone, "that course is so hard you have to have an angle or two. If it gets any harder, they're going to have to give S&H Green Stamps to get anybody to take it next year." With that he faded out of the room.

Finally I heard Moonbeam's sorority sisters rolling her down the steps. When she waddled into the parlor, she was daintily gnawing on a sandwich—a side of beef between two pieces of bread.

"Where would you like to go?" I asked, helping her with her tent-sized coat.

"Let's go to the Krystal," she giggled. "I just love that chili and those chocolate-covered donuts...yum!"

The girls who work at the Krystal are pretty fast operators, but they were no match for Moonbeam. Three of them went into a state of nervous exhaustion before we finally filled up Mercer's bottomless pit.

"Let's stop by the fruit stand and get a little snack before we go in," she said, nibbling on a loaf of bread kept on her person at all times, in case of emergency.

Gad, what a glutton…but going with her does give me one claim to fame: I'm the only person on the Mercer campi who has a wall-to-wall girlfriend. (March 1957)

A DEDICATED PROFESSION

Ignominy and gloom were mine. Out of 165 seniors taking Senior Comprehensive Exams, I was the only failure. I knew I was making a mistake in my freshman year when I let my faculty advisor, Symington C. Frump (often erroneously referred to as Pfsstron Liverkowcstein, a great Irish birdwatcher), talk me into majoring in Chinese. What a comprehensive! Several people turned in blank papers and got better grades than I did.

Fear was mine when I opened the post office box and found a note from Dean Featherfelt Shaftwell on his official black-bordered stationery requesting my immediate presence in his office.

I raced up to his office and ran to the desk of the kindly old receptionist. Trying to appear casual, I leaned on her desk and gasped, "Where is Dean Shaftwell?"

"Who am I, Inspector Keen, tracer of missing persons?" she countered, smashing my fingers with a sawed off fungo bat which she had cleverly concealed under her desk.

The bleeding had just about stopped when Dean Shaftwell opened the door to his chambers and beckoned me in. Dean Shaftwell is an impeccable dresser. Many think he was the first to bring the Ivy League look to Mercer. This, however, is not quite true. He does wear Ivy League clothes, but they are the same clothes he wore as an undergraduate at Slippery Rock State Teachers College in 1921—the style is just coming back.

I tipped quietly into his lavish office, the walls of which were papered with threatening letters he had received during his tenure as dean.

"Sit down, lad," he said.

"Thank you," I said, making a low curtsy and seating myself on the spot indicated on the floor.

"Well, it certainly is a lovely day."

"Indeed," I agreed, "twelve inches of rain since lunch."

"Well, enough of this pantheistic prattle," he screamed, slashing me across the face with his rubber hose. "You know why you're here, Clutchmeyer?"

"Yes," I lied, trying to appear nonchalant as I attempted to force my nose back into position.

"You are the only person in the history of this noble body of learning," he paused here to face Penfield and salaam thrice, "who has ever flunked a senior comprehensive exam. You will never," he continued, "be able to hold a regular, respectable position in the outside."

"Woe is me," I loudly lamented, attempting to slash my wrists on one of the many shafts which hung around his office.

"Here, here, child, I am your friend. Don't do anything rash that would mess up your life...or my office. Yes, there is another way...."

"Pray tell, what is that?" I asked.

"You can be a college professor!" he screamed, delighted at the prospect. "Think of it, Willard...$33 a month to start and a nickel a week raise every time Armistice Day falls on Sunday."

"Not really!" I exclaimed.

"Not only that," he added, "you can rent one of the faculty apartments for $325 a month. Of course, you will have to pay your own utilities, upkeep, and furnish doors and window panes."

"Gad," I mumbled, amazed at the good deal offered to scholarly profs who I thought heretofore lived in rented rooms and old soldiers' homes. "I may consider it."

"There are, of course, certain rules that the University expects all faculty members to follow: They must have no more than two suits, one of which must be tweed, baggy and at all times unpressed. It also speaks well for the teacher if one of the suits is spotted and stained, while the other must be dark and shiny. This suit may be worn to Faculty-Trustee frolics and public executions. Also, professors will not, I say will not, attend any chapel programs. I don't mind telling you, Willard," said the congenial Dean as he dusted his desktop with his peruke, "we catch a lot of professors violating the most fundamental rules. One person last year taught a course for three quarters without changing textbooks!"

"You don't mean it?" I asked, in obvious disbelief.

"Yes," he said, "and not only that, one undedicated instructor had the gall to pass more than half of his class! You can do it, Willard. Think about it and, in the meantime, practice mumbling. You speak much too distinctly for a college professor."

My heart beat periodically as I raced out of Dean Shaftwell's office and down to the Salvation Army store to buy a toga suitable for teaching purposes. (October 1957)

ANOTHER GAY PROGRAM

It was just last Friday and I was tipping gaily across our campi to chapel being closely followed by a large white dog that had confused me for a squirrel. I entered the inner sanctum a few moments late but, after being beaten good-naturedly about the head and face with a clipboard by the chapel checker, I was allowed to take my seat.

My fellow students were all reading newspapers in a half-hearted attempt to conceal their joy and enthusiasm in being allowed to come to chapel. A few pew mates cursed me cheerfully as I tropped across their feet to my space.

I had no sooner eased into my seat when the curtains parted and, after a brief organ fanfare, Dean Featherfelt Shaftwell slithered onto the stage and, with a wave of his hand, dismissed his two bodyguards. Smiling at the chorus of hisses and boos which greeted him and dodging an occasional soft drink bottle, he began:

"Students, it is with no little pleasure that I introduce to you today our Chapel speaker, who, too poor to go to school, graduated from Mercer in 1936. Ah, 1936," reminisced the Dean, "that wonderful, wonderful year. The year Gertrude Smederle, clad only in the contents of a large can of Snowdrift, swam the English

Channel is eleven hours and fifteen minutes, only to find upon reaching the French coast that she could have made the trip in a boat in less than forty-five minutes. The year electricity was discovered in Tennessee. The year William S. Hart was released from Twentieth Century Fox for selling whiskey to the Indians. The year Willard X. Clutchmyer, father of Mercer student Willard C. Clutchmyer, was admitted into evidence by Clarence Darrow in the Scopes Monkey Trial.

"An interesting sidelight on that Gertrude Smederle incident. Upon landing on the French coast she was denied admittance into the country because the beaches were so crowded that she was not allowed to come out of the water in her nude state. In a fit of pique, she returned to England only to find that after swimming for twenty-four hours, her passport was so soggy and illegible that she could not get back into the country. Well, there she was, a woman without a country, so to speak, and to the best of my recollection, there she remained, treading water in the English Channel, from 1936 to 1941, when she was torpedoed by a German U-boat. But I digress," laughed the Dean. "Our speaker, as I said…."

Before the Dean would continue, a redheaded math major leapt from his seat and cried, "A pox upon this tyranny! I'm Catholic and I refuse to go to the chapel on Fridays!"

"Pray tell me why," said the Dean in obvious consternation.

"We're not supposed to have baloney on Friday," rejoined the carrot-topped lad as he smiled and acknowledged the applause of the student body. His enjoyment was short-lived, however, as two of the Dean's men clouted him on the head with a starched sock from the Mercer laundry and dragged him from the arena.

"To continue," rasped the Dean as he lifted his peruke to mop a few beads of perspiration from the Marlboro tattoo located on his dome, "our speaker is one of our country's leading anarchists and has been practicing nepotism in Crisp County for the last five years. It was through his courageous efforts alone that fluoridation of the Locust Grove, Georgia, city water supply was prevented. Our speaker is a lawyer and his record, with the exception of two convictions for attempting to bribe jurors and a battery charge which is still pending, is unblemished. You might say he stands on his record."

A student in front of me, covering his mouth with a *Mad* comic, shouted, "If I had his record, I'd stand on it too!" The words had scarcely left his mouth before the Dean's two men, Marge and Gower, hustled the student from the chapel, beating him senseless with an esophagus tube.

"Without further ado," shouted the Dean, "I give you Waldo LeCompton Gnuzz, or, as he is sometimes called, Charles (Chuck) Starkweather."

Gnuzz bowed several times and acknowledged the applause, all of which was coming from Dean Shaftwell. He began, "Students, law students and faculty...." He paused to look toward the faculty section, which was completely empty save for Professor Swathmore Senile who, in 1943 upon hearing that faculty salaries were being raised from $19 to $21 a month, went into a coma and never recovered.

"I, too, have been sitting where you are now sitting, and I know how it is. As a matter of fact, if the administration hadn't discovered in 1935 that my fraternity had an eighteen-year-old housemother, you lads might have fraternity houses today. And then there was the time in 1932 when we kidnapped the Dean of Men, stripped him down to his garish long underwear, and threw him out of a speeding automobile onto the Wesleyan campus during the midst of a May Day celebration and the...."

Before he could finish the anecdote, the Dean burst up to the rostrum and shouted, "We interrupt this program to bring you a special news bulletin: The Mercer weight-lifting P.E. class, a subsidiary of Alpha Hernia weight-lifting fraternity, has been hired to be models for before pictures in Charles Atlas ads!"

The students, seizing this as an excuse to break up chapel, rushed out carrying Rudolph Rupture, captain of the Mercer weight lifters, out of the chapel. Rudolph, despite the cold weather, was garbed in a T-shirt which was three sizes too small. (May 1959)

WILLARD MAKES THE TEAM

Ecstasy and exuberance were mine to have and hold last week. I was standing in the Tattnall Tech post office trying to look nonchalant as I casually plucked lint from my navel, pausing to smile now and then at a few pitiful faculty members as they milled about waiting to claim CARE parcels sent them every month by a group of well-meaning Polish refugees.

I'm sure it was Friday because I was looking at the Wednesday package list on the bulletin board when, if I may borrow a line coined by that famous poet, patriot and statesman, Ezra Pound, "…my heart leapt up when I beheld" on the board a notice asking that all candidates for varsity sports repair immediately to the MU gym.

"Eureka!" I cried, causing a badminton major, Thurston Eureka, to look quizzically in my direction. "At last, a chance to display my latent athletic prowess!"

I rushed to the gym, pausing only to stop by the Co-op for a strength-giving Heath bar. In my childlike anxiety and enthusiasm, I placed my nickel on the glass-topped counter and was bitten on the arm in three places by the ever-popular cashier, Ima Crabbe. "Put the money in the plastic dish next time," she screamed good-naturedly, as I hurried off licking my wounds.

I went inside the clammy gym and tipped up to a boy who was playfully punching a bag. "Pray tell me where is the coach," said I. The bag, who turned out to be the boy's girlfriend, spoke up, "Do I look like an information booth, you jerk?"

Frightened, I darted upstairs and into the office of Head Coach and Athletic Director Knute Sweatsuit, who was cracking pistachio nuts with his teeth. Seeing me enter, he placed his teeth in his mouth and smiled broadly. "Well, lad, what can we do for you?"

"I just want to be a small part of the glorious Mercer sports scene," I cried. "Mercer! Mercer! Zip boom bah!"

The coach, obviously moved, brushed away a tear and we stood there for a moment, not trusting ourselves to speak. Finally he said, "Before this school de-emphasized sports and put the money into a retirement fund for old chapel speakers, I would have gladly booted you out of this office, but now I'm desperate. Only four boys have turned out for baseball this year, and three of them are right-handed first basemen. Our sports program wasn't always like it is now," he said. "At one time the name Mercer struck fear into the hearts of coaches from Agnes Scott to Alexander II.

"I'll give you a brief resume: Mercer was founded in 1921 by Arthur and Kathryn Murray as a dancing school for retarded high school graduates. The school prospered and enjoyed mild success until one day in 1926 Kathryn caught Arthur smiling at a well-turned coed. In a jealous rage, she thrashed him within an inch of his life. Legend has it that since that day Arthur has refused to smile at anyone and that dancing has been banned on the Mercer campi.

"But more about MU sports of days gone by. Who'll ever forget plucky little Claude Guano, who was perhaps one of college football's greatest one-legged punters. Then in 1931 we had Wilt 'The Stilt' Sforza, who holds the SEC basketball record for free throws missed by a left-handed center in a protest game played at night on a dirt court. When Sforza set this record, a group of cheering students immediately retired his jersey by locking it in the trophy case in the library. In their enthusiasm and glee, they neglected to take Sforza out of the jersey, and he remained there until the summer of 1943 when the case was opened so that the trophies could be given to a wartime scrap drive.

"Mercer was also active in aquatic sports in the early '30s. I'll never forget the Mercer University-University of Georgia diving meet held in 1934 at the indoor pool in Athens. Mercer's star, Johnny Winesmeller, raced off the high board over one hundred feet in the air and, in one spectacular dive, did a double somersault, a triple reverse twist, a jackknife and a swan dive. He would have undoubtedly won the meet had he not missed the pool by a scant three feet. In that very same meet, Mercer's LaSaza Gnuzz set a new world's record by remaining under water for four hours and thirty-six minutes but was disqualified when the judges found he had drowned.

"I'm not bitter, though," asserted the kindly mentor. "I know that the financial picture here hasn't been a good one. In 1938, for instance, all faculty members received, in lieu of a salary, an all-expenses-paid trip to Beersheba Baptist Campground in scenic Rabun Gap, Georgia. But enough of this, lad; have you had any experience in athletics?"

"Well," I confessed, "I was on the first-string basketball team of Bowdon High in '53."

"First string?" said the coach in obvious disbelief.

"Yes," I replied curtly, "and not only that, our coach said if I had tried a little harder I might have made the boys' team."

"How is your physical condition?" he asked sadly.

"Jolly good," I exclaimed, "but I have been seeing spots before my eyes."

"Have you seen an oculist?" he asked.

"No, just spots," I answered, winking my good eye at him.

"I mean, have your eyes been checked lately?" he moaned.

"No," I confessed, "they've always been green."

"I give up!" shrieked the coach, running his hand over his smooth dome, searching for hair to pull. "Here, take this uniform and report for practice tomorrow."

Crying with joy, I pressed the dirty uniform to my trembling breast and, through my tears, I read the name of the buyer and sponsor of the uniform. In big orange letters the back of my shirt bore the words Woman's Christian Temperance Union. (October 1958)

YOUNGER LAWYERS SECTION NEWSLETTER

IT'S A FAMILY TRADITION

To recount the life and career of Charles Driebe would make Horatio Alger twitch in unrestrained envy. It is the story of a boy who progressed from a poverty-stricken childhood (allegedly the first piece of white bread he ever saw was thrown from the back of a C.C.C. truck) to President of one of the most powerful legal organizations on this continent—the Younger Lawyers Section.

Unwanted as child, Driebe is now wanted in three states and Canada. His first contact with the law was at the age of two when he was the center of a bitter custody battle between his parents. Ultimately his father lost the case and was forced to take custody.

Driebe's family background is steeped in legal tradition. Two of his cousins can boast of never having missed an episode of *Perry Mason*; an older brother was introduced into evidence by the defense in the Scopes Monkey Trial; a distant relation, a member of the U.S. Supreme Court, made legal history by declaring World War II unconstitutional; and a maiden aunt works quietly in Catoosa County circulating a petition to free Sacco and Vanzetti.

His love of politics is explained by the fact that his mother was frightened during gestation while attending an Alf Landon rally. Entering politics at an early age, he was nominated for

Village Idiot and won by a landslide. He abandoned a lifelong urge to become a Notary Public after failing the exam several times and finally turned to law. "It was either that or go to work," he explained.

Too poor to go to Emory and refusing to go to Mercer because of a deep-seated aversion to snake handling (at that time it was a required course at Mercer even for those not studying the ministry), Driebe enrolled at Georgia Law School and graduated in seven years.

True to his code of self-sufficiency, he worked his way through law school selling Avon products. "I didn't make too many sales," he said modestly, "but I always smelled good." (*Younger Lawyers Section*, August 1963)

IS THAT REALLY HIS NAME?

Many think Cicero Garner was named after the great Roman orator. Actually Garner was named after a small town in Illinois. He was born in 1936 but his parents were too stunned to call him anything for almost six years. Finally, in desperation, they chose his name by throwing a dart at a map of the United States. The procedure was so satisfactory that it was followed in naming Cicero's two younger brothers—Daytona Beach and Lake Huron.

Cicero enjoyed as normal a childhood as possible for an overweight child in a rural community who is forced by his parents to wear corduroy knickers year round. Though his denim-clad playmates scoffed at the whistling produced by his corduroys, Garner soon changed their scorn to amazement when he learned that by varying his gait he could produce almost all of the popular tunes of the day. He went on to win the Original Burke County Amateur Hour contest under the name "C. Garner and his Syncopated Plus Fours."

After several smash engagements entertaining at the top local clubs—Moose, VFW and Order of the Eastern Star—it was obvious that young Garner had a future in show business. His parents, however, sought a more normal life for the lad and sent him to military school where, despite some difficulties in obtaining uniforms (they had to be ordered from Lane Bryant), he excelled.

Garner agonized for some time over which college to attend, but his problem was abruptly solved when he won a scholarship to Emory University as a door prize at a Methodist revival meeting.

It was at Emory that he met a beautiful exchange student from Colombia, South America. Unable to speak English, she stopped him to ask directions and, through an unbelievable combination of linguistic difficulties, misunderstanding and, some say, deliberate misrepresentations, she found herself married to the wily Garner. With resignation, which is sometimes characteristic of those whom fate has crushed, Mrs. Garner attempted to make the best of the situation and embarked upon a reciprocal tutoring program whereby she would learn English and Cicero, Spanish. At this writing, Mrs. Garner speaks fluent English with a Burke County accent, while her husband's total Spanish vocabulary consists of si, no, and Caesar Romero.

By holding his breath and rigorously teasing the few hairs remaining on his broad, sloping forehead, Garner manages through the day to create the illusion of a distinguished young attorney. By night, Garner sits at home eating Ry-Crisps and puzzling over the unanswerable question which confounds all with falling hair—"If bald men are so virile, why does Mr. Clean have pierced ears?" (*Younger Lawyers Section*, October 1967)

WHO SHAVED THE CHIHUAHUA?

In Geneva, Illinois, at precisely 8:26 p.m. on April 23, 1940, while all America was glued to their radios listening to the Ted Mack Original Amateur Hour as a frantic unemployed yam grower from Demopolis, Alabama, played "Under the Double Eagle" while clog dancing on an electric whoopee cushion, Roy William Ide III was born to poor but proud parents. This event was to change their lives: while they continued to be poor, they were never proud again.

Struck in infancy with what was later diagnosed as terminal diaper rash, the soggy young Ide was rushed to Greenville, South Carolina, in the hope that a milder climate might give relief. The fortuitous discovery of Clearasil (developed from a mold found under the bangs of American teenagers) brought Ide's condition under control and, except for having to practice law standing up, it has proved no great hardship.

Ide enjoyed as normal a childhood as was possible for one prematurely bald at age ten. Even this handicap was turned to good advantage as it led to a full scholarship to Washington & Lee when Ide became the DAR's 1957 winner of the "Y.A. Tittle Look-alike Contest."

Infuriated by the charge that W&L was a party school, Ide sought out the most challenging courses available, earning a C+ average in folk dancing and shop. Literati at W&L still recall Ide's brilliant senior thesis, "Over One Hundred Really Good Knock-Knock Jokes."

Rejected by Virginia Law School because of low scores in arrogance, the irrepressible Ide managed to attend three years as class mascot while posing as a hairless Chihuahua with a thyroid condition. The only aftereffect of this period is Ide's inability to travel by automobile unless his head is hanging, slack tongued, out the window.

Ide is married to a lovely Sears Roebuck heiress who, while on a routine inspection tour of the Ponce de Leon store, discovered Ide salivating over the corset section of the Fall and Winter catalog. They recently moved into a modest six-bedroom home in Atlanta which is an authentic reproduction of the Alamo Plaza Motel in Tallapoosa, Georgia.

Ide spends his spare time reading Nancy Drew books and preparing a lawsuit against a social club as a result of an injury he sustained while going to his car following a New Year's party (someone stepped on his hand).

Ide is a member of the well-known firm of Whitelipped & Trembling, where he specializes in non-billable time. Charges by disgruntled partners that he is a "committee junkie" appear to have some substance. He is Chairman of the Younger Lawyers Section Committee on Conjugal Visits for Associates and founded the State Bar Committee on No-Fault Pregnancy. On noting 1972 statistics that Atlanta led the nation in increase of murder and V.D., Ide leaped into action, forming a committee to attack both problems by attempting to persuade murderers to kill only those with V.D. (*Younger Lawyers Section*, January 1973)

NEVER TALK BACK TO A WITCH DOCTOR

The *Guinness Book of World Records* contains many important Georgia references. In 1917 an abandoned kidney stone weighing almost fourteen pounds was discovered behind the Amoco station in Dewey Rose, Georgia. The discoverers of the famous stone (now a part of the permanent collection of the Museum of Fine Arts in Marietta) were led to their find by tracing a series of mysterious screams. In 1922, Mrs. Sarah Mae Spleen of Chatsworth, Georgia, in the grip of what she claimed to be a divine visitation (later diagnosed as a spastic colon), produced the world's ugliest chenille bedspread. In 1935, a team of South Georgia physicians working with a research grant from the WPA pronounced Joe Bob Bledsoe (the "Hahira Hunchback") perfectly normal after x-rays revealed that every morning for forty-six years he had been buttoning his collar to his fly. And in 1953, a full-grown teenaged boy, A. Felton Jenkins, was discovered in Madison, Georgia, with a size three and seven-eighths head.

Who could have guessed that one day this young lad would overcome his cruel handicap and rise to power as President of the world-powerful Georgia Younger Lawyers Section?

Jenkins's story was brought to light by a cub sports reporter from Atlanta who was in Madison covering the annual Morgan

County Track, Field, and Hog Flogging competition. Heartstrings across the nation were tugged when the wire services carried his account of how plucky young Jenkins, faced with failure at football because of lack of head gear, fashioned a helmet from a rubber band and an Ipana toothpaste cap and went on to win regional honors.

Entering college on a Robert Ripley scholarship, young Jenkins thrived in the demanding atmosphere of academic excellence which, then and now, characterizes the University of Georgia. In 1959, he was one of five Georgia freshmen to win the coveted "I Can Dress Myself" badge. Other students, jealous of his academic success and suspicious that such good grades could be achieved with such a small head, reported Jenkins to the Honor Council for cheating. Jenkins was completely exonerated, however, after exhaustive tests conducted at the School of Veterinary Medicine revealed that he had brains in his arm, neck, left shoulder and lunch pail.

Jenkins's undergraduate achievements peaked when he was tapped for membership in the highly secret Gridiron Society. This honor did not go to Jenkins's head for two reasons: first, it (his head, not the honor) was too small, and second, the Society was so secret that Jenkins was never told of his membership. He learned of it only by chance many years later after having the steam room attendant at the YMCA arrested for making improper advances, only to learn at the arraignment hearing that the defendant was a brother Gridiron trying to administer the secret grip.

Jenkins was active in extra-curricular activities at Georgia, where he originated the annual Leo Gorcey film festival, tap-danced and twirled baton, ran a detoxification center at the Phi Delta Theta house, and played "Mr. Germ" in the Health Club's production of "Don't Touch That Thing, You Don't Know Where It's Been."

His success is best demonstrated by the tribute other YLS politicos pay him in emulating his handicap for political gain. The current President-elect of the Section, Robert Brinson, while possessing a normal size head, handily defeated all opposition by claiming (and proving) that he had the smallest brain in the race. The newly elected Secretary, an obscure Atlanta subway attorney, William Ide, swept into office by craftily reducing the size of his head through the simple expedient of removing all of his hair. "Well, you know," says Jenkins (who is an articulate and stunning phrase-maker), "imitation is the sincerest form of flattery they is." (*Younger Lawyers Section*, July 1972)

BUT DOCTOR, HAVE YOU HUGGED YOUR LAWYER TODAY?

I was a bit suspicious when my secretary of twenty years, Yvonne "I-didn't-go-to-the-Marsh-Business-College-for-three-months-to-learn-how-to-fetch-coffee-for-you" McMillan, told me that folks from the *Journal of the Medical Association of Georgia* were trying to get in touch with me. Sensing my anxiety, she said soothingly, "Don't worry, they probably just want you to pose for a few photos on an upcoming article on stretch marks."

Notwithstanding her reassuring speculation, it occurred to me that these weren't the best of times for doctors and lawyers in terms of professional relations, and I certainly wasn't eager to put my head in the lion's mouth gratuitously.

When I finally worked up the courage to return the call left by a member of the magazine's publications committee, the distinguished surgeon, J. Rupert "Thumbs" Tillabaugh, I was informed that they wanted a "light-hearted piece that might bring a smile to the lips of readers of the *Journal*." I expressed some reluctance to the good doctor about my ability to lighten or enliven the *Journal*, but he urged me to review a few copies before saying no. After poring over some scintillating expositions on fascinating subjects ranging from "Symptoms of Irritable Bowel Syndrome" and "The Efficacy of Measuring Bone Mineral Density in Asymptomatic Women: A Preliminary Report" to "Clinical Management of Endocrine Disorders," I decided that perhaps a bit of froth certainly couldn't wreak any permanent havoc and might well punch up the *Journal* for a brief moment.

Filing with Dr. Tillabaugh in advance a caveat that all of my writings were accompanied by some contraindications, such as acute fulminations from over-serious readers, oral foaming, involuntary spasms and sputtering on the part of the acutely dignified, and sphincter rigidity in those with known sensitivity to feeble attempts at humor, I finally agreed to attempt a piece for the *Journal*.

The thought that doctors (or those who often take themselves more seriously about being doctors than the doctors do themselves, that is, doctors' wives) might take offense at finding an intruder from the legal profession flopping about in the deep and serene waters of the *Journal* gave me some pause, but it was only momentary as I reasoned that I, as a municipal bond attorney, wasn't a *real* lawyer after all and thus could probably lay claim to more objectivity on the subject of professional relations than someone who actually tried and prosecuted lawsuits. After all, one of my litigator law partners, Byron "Whiplash" Attridge, once described municipal bond attorneys as "people with not enough personality to be tax lawyers but with too much personality to be CPAs."

As someone who has flogged himself around the state addressing Bar conventions and medical associations, I have indeed had an opportunity to give thoughtful reflection and temperate expression to the decline in cordiality between the two professions. Frankly, I believe that one of the root causes of this hostile quandary in which we find ourselves locked is a loss of self-esteem among members of both professions. Indeed, who can blame either profession for feeling a slight downward shift in dignity when we find on every cable television channel some huckster lawyer importuning the sick, lame, and halt (not to be confused with the small law firm in Marietta by the same name) to drop by for a free consultation on their legal woes, or see in every shopping center some docs in a box called the "24-Hour EmergiCenter, Ear Piercing Clinic and Video Rental." Perhaps a return to more dignified times when lawyers wore vests and doctors had unlisted phone numbers would be better for all of us. However, times change, and we must accommodate the change without getting too bitter and resentful about it all.

Of course, I can't speak about the sensitivities of physicians in terms of loss of self-esteem, but in the area of public relations, lawyers have long been notorious victims. Throughout history, they have been pilloried in song, verse, and print by an unforgiving and misunderstanding public. This has, at times, made them jealous and resentful of their brethren in the medical profession.

As a member of that beleaguered brotherhood at the Bar, I am always confounded as to why it is that in every public opinion poll ever taken, doctors, and specifically surgeons, are always right up there at the top of scientists, astronauts, and Mother Teresa, while lawyers find themselves in a knot at the bottom of the pile with used car salesmen, carnival geeks, chiropractors, and Congressmen. After all, the law was a noble and enduring profession when medicine involved little more than pulverizing frog eggs, lizard spleens, and yak antlers, and surgery was still primarily a sideline practiced by barbers.

Some have suggested as a cause for the widespread and notorious unpopularity of lawyers that there are simply too many of us and, indeed, this is becoming a growing theme for an unrelenting and sensationalist press. As I have said before in my newspaper column and from the stump, this notion is sheer nonsense. In point of fact, this country at present has only 750,000 lawyers, more or less, with the result that many people don't even have a lawyer of their own but are forced to share one. This is not only inefficient but, depending upon the particular lawyer, downright unsanitary.

No, even in olden days, when there were far fewer legal practitioners, there was an unreasoning prejudice against lawyers. The drafters of Georgia's original Charter provided that it was to be "a happy, flourishing colony...free from [as they diplomatically phrased it] the pest and scourge of mankind known as lawyers." Shakespeare's Dick the Butcher, reacting enthusiastically to Cade's Utopian vision, urged, "The first thing we do, let's kill all the lawyers." Carl Sandburg wrote with malicious and alliterative glee, "Why does the hearse horse snicker when he's hauling a lawyer away?" And even St. Luke (a known physician) took a gratuitous jab in Chapter 11, Verse 46, with "Woe unto ye lawyers also! For you load men with burdens hard to bear, and you yourselves do not touch the burdens with one of your fingers."

Every day seems to bring a new bad joke about lawyers, e.g., "What do you get when you cross a lawyer with a Godfather?" Answer: "Someone who makes you an offer you can't understand." Some weaker members of the legal profession actually crack under the strain of this bad press. I know a lawyer who drives a bread truck to and from his office in an attempt to prevent his neighbors from learning the true nature of his day job. Others, when confronted by their sobbing children who have been told by cruel and insensitive playmates that their parent is a lawyer, resort to guile and outright deception, telling their children they are really cocaine traffickers, members of the General Assembly, or proctologists.

I have long pointed out to lawyers everywhere that doctors are entirely different in this respect and have a much larger quotient of self-esteem. As one lawyer friend of mine recently observed, "It's refreshing to see how much faith doctors have in themselves, particularly in these troubled times when so many people believe in no God at all."

I tell lawyers that they can learn from practitioners of the healing arts in terms of self-respect. It's simply a matter of self-esteem and pride in their profession. Doctors are *proud* to be doctors. They have little signs on their automobile license plates advertising the fact that they are doctors. (This also permits them to park in spaces which would otherwise be reserved for handicapped people.) At movies, concerts, and cocktail parties, doctors happily proclaim their profession by wearing little beepers on their belts like old-time gunslingers. Some of the younger doctors, having noted that typewriter repairmen also wear these beepers, will often go to a public gathering with a stethoscope hanging casually from their pockets just to avoid any confusion. I have seen doctors show up at formal gatherings in black tie wearing reflectors on their noggins. This does convey a certain panache to an otherwise humdrum outfit.

Moreover, if doctors get into a situation that is so crowded that people are likely to notice neither the electronic beeper nor the dangling stethoscope—a football game, for example—they will simply have themselves paged. I've long advocated having lawyers paged at football games. I think it would help their images tremendously…"Lawyer 84, Lawyer 84, please call your office. You missed a mortgage when you checked that last title."

Actually, the doctors are now claiming that there are too many doctors as well. I'd be a little more inclined to accept that claim if all doctors listed their home telephone numbers. Moreover, you have to make an appointment months in advance to see many specialists, not to mention getting up all the credit references. If an unexpected client happens to wander into a lawyer's office, they not only see him right away but generally fall on him like a school of piranha in a feeding frenzy.

Frankly, my prescription to both lawyers and doctors is nothing more than the wisdom long embodied in Rule 5 of the Kansas General Assembly. This paradigm of good common sense was promulgated by the Kansas General Assembly around the turn of the last century and goes simply, "Don't take yourself so damn serious." I am persuaded that if practitioners in both professions would simply take themselves and each other a bit more lightly, we would have made a great first stride in getting the proverbial lion and the lamb to lie down together. But, in all fairness, I should pass along to doctors the admonition of that great American philosopher Ralph Waldo Emerson (I think it was he; it was either Emerson or Shecky Green), who said, "The lion and the lamb may lie down together, but the lamb isn't going to get a hell of a lot of sleep." (*Journal of the Medical Association of Georgia*, April 1988)

AND THE GREEDY SHALL INHERIT THE AIRWAVES

Television owes a towering debt of gratitude to the South. As New York's Great White Way is the breeding ground for so many talented folks in the world of entertainment, so is our Bible Belt the incubator for the swarm of TV preachers now infesting the airwaves. I think it was either Savonarola, St. Francis of Assisi, or the Reverend Ike who once said, "The Lord moves in mysterious ways his wonders to unfold." Evidence abounds to sustain the eternal verity of that well-known maxim, and we need dig no further for proof of the metaphysical pudding than to flip about the cable TV channels with a type-A remote-control device and check out the growing number of electronic evangelists who are swarming like heavenly moths to the bright video light. It is absolutely frightening to see just how mysteriously the Lord is in fact moving these days.

The old-fashioned church in the wildwood is rapidly giving way to an incredible array of electronic Elmer Gantrys cavorting all over the cable systems. On virtually every other notch you'll find a number of show-biz preachers competing for contributions from the sick and shut-in along with an amazing and cunning variety of space-age, plate-passing techniques.

Like programming on the network channels, they offer every possible format. Some adopt the Johnny Carson approach complete with guests and a jowly, over-appreciative, perpetually chuckling sidekick. Others have a mom-and-pop type approach with husband and wife evangelists taking on the devil and his allies in tag-team fashion. Still others appear in front of row on row of telephone volunteers and importune or shame their recliner-chair-bound parishioners to call in pledges much in the manner of a Jerry Lewis telethon.

There are a few of the traditional stand-up, Bible-thumping, fire-and-brimstone, old-school shouters who, when I was growing up in west Georgia, appeared in the streets or, in the high church variety, in canvas tents. These were known locally as "suck-back" preachers because of the great gulps of air they would ingest at the end of every sentence to both punctuate and sustain their soul-searing oratory.

These folks have always been around but television has given them a splendid new dimension. I can remember with great clarity a legendary saver of souls who operated in and around Bowdon, Georgia, during my youth, the Reverend Norman Vincent Jeter. He spoke in tongues, cured most illnesses not requiring immediate hospitalization by a firm laying on of hands and wrenching the believer's head about in circles, built a cinder-block sanctuary on the Alabama line, and made a fair to middlin' living through the fervent and frequent exhortation of the parishioners of his Fire Baptized, Holiness, No Makeup, Jewelry or Lewd Doings, Pentecostal Church of West Georgia, East Alabama and the Latter Day Saints. The Reverend Jeter gained national attention as a gospel singer while still a child. His tenor version of "Justice Called and Mercy Answered," while accompanying himself on the electric ocarina, still causes the LeFevre Family to twitch in collective and unrestrained envy. In his teens, Jeter left gospel music to become a full-time faith healer. Operating as "Oral (if I can feel 'em, I can heal 'em) Jeter," his practice was to loiter about the square in Carrollton and fall on infirmed passersby with alacrity.

With nothing more than an army surplus tent and several hundred funeral home fans, Jeter staged a spectacular revival on the banks of the Little Tallapoosa River, climaxing it by baptizing more than three hundred people, almost all of them by force. I am certain that the Reverend Jeter would be a soaring superstar in the evangelical Nielsens if he were alive today. Regrettably, his talent for laying on of hands had some unfortunate secular aspects, and he was made a martyr by an irate husband with a strong sense of betrayal and a stout two-by-four.

Like the Reverend Jeter, many of his modern-day equivalents operating on the airwaves can cure ailments where medical science has failed. Viewing the mysterious miracles wrought by these marvels on the obscure cable channels does, like listening to politicians or watching Live Atlanta Wrestling, require some mild suspension of doubt and logic but, as the farmer who was once asked if he believed in "infant baptism" replied, "Believe it? Why, I've seen it with my own eyes!" such is the case for those of us who assiduously follow the late-night doings of those towering spiritual presences who inhabit the cable TV ministries.

The Reverend Ernest Angley, trussed up in what appears to be an endless succession of rainbow-hued polyester creations by Supphose, will, right before your very eyes, heal a variety of illnesses. I personally have seen him exorcise diabetes, shortness of breath, alcoholism, neuritis, and neuralgia from the bodies of the faithful by the simple expedient of popping them in the middle of their foreheads with his open palm. The result is literally staggering. The afflicted are momentarily stunned, as if dubbed with a cattle prod, and reel or flop backwards into the arms of Angley's assistants. Like those in the medical profession, the healers appear to me to specialize, and I would judge the Reverend Angley to be most effective in the area of restoring hearing. Many are the times that I have witnessed a disoriented soul led into his presence and seen the afflicted's hearing restored.

In my quest for spiritual succor on the airways, I recently flipped into a new format in the person of two fat, singing spiritualists. I use the term "fat" as opposed to "stout," "plump," "overweight," or "obese" because these hearty healers looked as though they should be rigged with curb feelers. They regaled the TV audience with an anecdote about a recent healing experience that had given the reverend a moment of apprehension. He said laughingly that a bald woman came before them for healing when, out of the blue (where else?), his spiritual sidekick announced to the woman that she had heard the Lord speak and the Lord had said the woman's hair would be restored. This, said the Reverend Arbuckle (not his real name,) surprised him in that he had not heard the Lord speak, and he was even further agitated by his wife's assurance to the woman that the Lord had specified that her hair would be restored in three days. "Tell them why you were worried," laughed his wife good-naturedly. "Well," he chuckled, his ample dewlaps literally aquiver with merriment, "we were going to be in that town for three days." Fortunately, the story had a happy ending. The woman showed up three days later with "fuzz" on her noggin, and six months later they encountered the woman's mother who assured them that her daughter was now fully fuzzed. While I had no reason to question their claims about the hair coming back, I did have a fleeting feeling that if the Lord could heal the bald, He would do well to lop a couple of hundred pounds off of His massive messengers.

I would not presume to question the sincerity of any in this ever-increasing phalanx of preachers and prophets, but I have noticed with some concern that the road to salvation appears to be paved with cash love offerings continually exhorted from the faithful. That there is big money in these enterprises is evidenced by the fact that some of the preachers spend as much time fending off the Internal Revenue Service as they do shearing their flocks. They are bringing in the sheaves in flat cars, often more than the budget of many small churches. And the pitches are enhanced with a frightening range of emotions which can switch from joy and exhilaration to tears and bleak despair in the bat of a long, feathery, mascara-laden eyelash. In many cases the Lord will actually speak to the TV preacher, making recommendations as to the precise amounts expected of the faithful.

Where will it all end?

My guess is that when the major networks find out how much dough is involved, *Dallas* will be replaced by the *PTL Club* and J. R. will have to be doing postgraduate work at Oral Roberts U.

There is even a rumor that President Reagan has a secret plan to get the Right Reverend Jerry Falwell (and it is hard to imagine a reverend more right) to further trample the line separating church and state by going on the air to raise money to reduce the federal deficit. I like it better than a tax hike.

I think what we're seeing is just the beginning. Even now, in the quiet of the evenings, I can hear the voices raising in the electronic church in the vale as they join together and sing, "Gimme That Prime Time Religion…." (April 1985)

LADIES, LEAVE YOUR RAINCOATS AT HOME; MERCER IS A PARTY SCHOOL NOW

At the breakfast table one morning recently while attempting to get my heart jump-started with a cup of my wife's fabulous coffee ("Mix one level teaspoon of Maxim with one cup of boiling water; stir briskly. Serves one."), I was bowled over by a dispatch in the morning paper revealing that my alma mater, Mercer University, has been designated by *Playboy* magazine as No. 9 in its annual survey of the top forty party colleges. With a center of gravity that has tended to get larger and lower with advancing years, I am generally regarded as one who is difficult to bowl over, but this bit of news was simply too much even for my growing equilibrium.

My mind reeled with troubled thought as to how things could have changed so since my undergraduate days when Mercer was a cloister of rectitude, right thinking, and scholarship. From its earliest days it was a paradigm of piety and erudition. Matters had not changed much by 1954 when my parents took me to Bean's Drugstore that served as the bus station for Bowdon, Georgia, and put me on a southbound Greyhound with a large lapel sign saying, "Put this boy off in Macon."

Looking back, I can say without reservation that in 1954 Mercer had about as much chance of getting on anyone's top party college list as Dr. Ruth has of getting named dean of women at Oral Roberts University.

The attitude of the school's administration toward any activity beyond study and character development was nothing short of reactionary. By way of example, coeds were permitted to wear shorts to gym classes but, while they were traversing the campus or otherwise in public view, they were required to wear a raincoat lest their young bodies excite lascivious thought on the part of leering law students. (The advantage this rule gave the Wesleyan College students during the bathing-suit portion of the Miss Macon Contest was inestimable.)

The 1954 student handbook, in a rule that would now be thought sexist, provided that, "No female student shall be permitted to smoke in public unless, of course, she is actually on fire."

Stricter still was the rigid and almost pathological prohibition against dancing on campus. To make it sound more insidious, the administration characterized it as "mixed dancing," and any such carnal activity was absolutely proscribed. As editor-in-chief of the hard-hitting, world-famous *Mercer Cluster* (the journalistic incubator for Fourth Estate luminaries such as Bert Struby, Jack Tarver, and Reg Murphy, the last of whom left Atlanta under cover of darkness in the trunk of an automobile), I began what was to become a lifetime affliction of intemperate railing in print when I injected myself into the eye of a theological hurricane by suggesting that, contrary to the then-prevailing view of the Baptist hierarchy, there was no solid clinical data to support their notion that the box step was contributing to the decline of Western civilization or that it led inevitably to that pernicious activity described in Deuteronomy as "begetting."

Such rank apostasy invariably provoked paroxysms of consternation in the ranks of the administration officials and among the ministerial students who swarmed the campus in great numbers and, once again, I would find myself No. 1 on the Mercer Prayer List maintained from week to week by those good and pious scholars. It's worth noting in the context of partying that those students' idea of a good time was to go down to the city jail and sing hymns to the inmates. The inmates were finally successful in getting the practice enjoined as a violation of their constitutional rights against cruel and unusual punishment.

That in a mere thirty years the institution could have drifted so far from its charted moral course will (taking into account that Mercer still is, to borrow Dr. Ferrol Sams's marvelously apt expression, "Baptist to the bone") surely cause in some of the righteous ranks feelings of dread and loathing and provoke some mild moaning, gnashing of teeth, and renting of garments (Mercerians are notorious for renting garments, particularly tuxedos, which only a few of them can afford to own). But as for this aging rebel who fulminated so fulsomely and ineffectively against the rigid puritanism of the '50s, my honest reaction to the *Playboy* news was, "Where did we go right?" (December 1986)

YOU'VE NOTHING TO LOSE BUT SERVING SUGGESTIONS

Introspection is often a painful process and, I must confess, it gives me more than a little chagrin to admit that in the past I have not been as sensitive to every aspect of the feminist movement as I might have been.

For the last ten years or so, I have been largely unmoved and insensitive to the need expressed by a growing number of women to "get out of the house," "find themselves," or "go to law school," but that lack of sensitivity on my part is now a thing of the past.

My transformation came in a blinding flash of light while I was standing up the other evening at our kitchen counter making some potato chips disappear. (It is a well-known scientific fact that food eaten in a standing position metabolizes almost twice as fast as the same size portions ingested while seated.) So as to avoid responding to shrieks from my wiry wife that I was going to "ruin my supper," I feigned distraction by reading the label on a package of brown 'n' serve French rolls.

I had gone into the text on the package only a short distance before my gorge began to rise in indignation as I realized in what low esteem housewives were held by the supercilious purveyors of these rolls. The package indicated straightaway that the bakers of these particular rolls considered housewives to be cretinous creatures who must be led by the hand through the simplest of tasks.

Under the caption "Serving Suggestions" there appeared the following:

No. 1: "Remove from bag before heating." Surely, I thought, there are no housewives bright enough to read who would insert the rolls and the bag in an oven.

Instruction No. 2 adjured the confused cooks to "preheat oven to 425 degrees."

Suggestion No. 3 was to "place rolls on ungreased baking sheet." At this point I wondered if a parenthetical warning should be added alerting the housewife not to confuse a baking sheet with a bed sheet.

Suggestion No. 4 was "brush tops with melted butter" and, this time, a parenthetical "before or after baking" was thoughtfully added. It occurred to me that even if they had left off Suggestion No. 1 about removing the rolls from the bag before heating, the average housewife would figure this out by the time she got to brushing the tops with melted butter. On the other hand, I guess these bakers didn't want to take anything for granted.

Suggestion No. 5 said to bake seven to ten minutes, serve and enjoy. This seemed like good advice to me and couldn't, by any reasonable person, be thought to be patronizing. However, just after this instruction there appeared in bold letters yet another warning…"DO NOT PUT THIS BAG IN OVEN."

Perhaps those of you who have not achieved my level of sensitivity will suggest that the instructions were gender neutral as men in this enlightened age can often be found browning and serving with the best of them, particularly those super-sensitive, simpering wimps on *Thirtysomething* who, every time their wife sighs or focuses on infinity, will furrow a husbandly brow and, in a voice oozing with concern, say, "Honey, are you OK?"

Well, it may be true that the drafters of the serving suggestions didn't have the softer sex in mind in promulgating their overweening advisories, but I can't imagine a manufacturer beginning instructions on how to start a lawn mower, for example, by specifying, "First, take lawn mower out of crate."

As a newly awakened Sensitive Person, I for one bitterly resent the vision of womanhood suggested by the sellers of these brown 'n' serve rolls—a sleepy, slack-jawed, glassy-eyed hausfrau who, still in her chenille bathrobe at suppertime, stumbles into the kitchen after an arduous day watching soap operas and game shows, needing to be taken by the hand and instructed as to how to perform the simplest of tasks.

Women of the world, unite! You have nothing to lose but your "serving suggestions." There is no good reason why you should suffer such scorn, ridicule, and public abuse. After all, you're not the vice president of the United States.

"Enough," as Elizabeth Taylor said in declining a recent marriage proposal, "is enough." (August 1989)

DEMOCRACY ON THE RUN

Aside from the sheer dedication, heroics, and exhilaration from the front to the back of the Peachtree Road Race, the most amazing aspect of that massive, mobile, and self-propelled spectacle is how genuinely democratic it is. It's as though the Masters Golf Tournament invited the world to play and swarms of Avon ladies, plumbers, chiropractors, Shriners, and transmission specialists grabbed random implements and began whacking the hell out of the August National.

I should have realized that there was absolutely nothing selective about the event after seeing the prerace photo in the newspapers over the caption "Come Run the Peachtree Road Race with *Atlanta Constitution* Editor Hal Gulliver." The picture, which could have passed at Nuremberg as atrocity evidence, features the spindle-shanked Gulliver in a strap undershirt (reminiscent of what still passes for semi-formal attire in his native Valdosta) and a headband that he doubtless intended an as athletic affectation, but which I suspected as evidence that he had simply closed the car door on his head again (a justification management has often used by way of explanation for his columns).

Notwithstanding this ample warning of the totally democratic nature of our swelling rite, I was simply flabbergasted (just the right word) by the spectacle. Having never seen it before, I expected something like a race or an athletic event and, for the first one thousand or so of the participants who moved serenely by, it thus appeared. But then! Great God! Around the bend a stampede appeared which would have convinced the unknowing that some sinister force had flushed everyone out of Marietta in their underwear and was herding them south with electric cattle prods. Twelve thousand sweating taxpayers huffing along in attitudes ranging from sheer desperation to low comedy.

There appeared to be four basic categories: the runners, the joggers, the lurchers, and, finally, the flotsam and jetsam division. The last category was by far the most colorful and courageous contingent. It featured grim and sweating housewives looking as though they had just gone over the wall at a European Health Spa and didn't intend to be taken back alive; geriatric marvels wearing T-shirts proclaiming "These are my teeth too!"; a jogging juggler; and one particularly inspiring entry which looked as though 150 pounds of cellulite had been dropped from a high place onto a pair of sneakers—don't scoff, it was moving steadily. My favorite was one of those marathon walkers with a mincing gait which perpetually threatens to break into a full-blown skip. I offered even money that he wouldn't finish the race in under fifty minutes, and was quickly countered by a swarthy citizen in mirrored sunglasses who gave me nine-to-five that he wouldn't get past Pershing Point if any of the waiters at Chez Quiche spotted his syncopated strolling style.

It may be a race for the first hundred and it may be an athletic event for the next thousand or so; but I am convinced that Mel Brooks staged the rest of the affair and it is one of his best efforts. This is not to say that it isn't thoroughly worthwhile. It is a heroic challenge for every participant and a vicarious thrill for every spectator—not so thrilling, however, as to stimulate this flabby spectator to attempt anything more strenuous than getting up early to see it again next year.

If you haven't seen one, you ought to go while you can. Like Hula-Hoops, marathon dancing, and flagpole sitting, these things don't last forever. What passes for sanity inevitably—and for those who enjoy watching zany doings, regrettably—has a nasty way of reasserting itself. (July 1978)

EXPLICIT DR. RUTH JUST CAN'T COMPARE TO "BOB AND SALLY"

I don't know how many of you have been knocking around in the upper reaches of double-digit cable TV, but there are some weird things going on up there. I'm not talking about just the faith healers, the flabby wrestlers shouting imprecations, or the kung fu folks kicking each other silly; I'm talking about some really weird stuff. Specifically, I'm talking about a program featuring a Transylvanian Ma Kettle called "Dr. Ruth," who gives gratuitous and hard-core sexual advice to anyone who shows up or calls in.

This lascivious Lilliputian is the star of a show redundantly titled *Good Sex*. After just one viewing, it occurred to me that asking Dr. Ruth about good sex is like asking the Japanese for tips on World War II. I mean, I'm much more interested in Joan Collins's views on the subject. But there the diminutive doctor is, looking directly into the camera like Wendy's "Where's the Beef?" lady, and crooning things like "Vat I vant you to do is to buy a rubber jumpsuit, some schmall whips und a little trampoline and ven your husband comes homes at night…." It's enough to make the League of Decency tremble like a bird dog on the end of a diving board.

First of all, it's embarrassing to watch. It's like having your grandmother take you aside to tell you about the birds and the bees.

In the second place, at the risk of being characterized as a casualty of the sexual revolution, I think this whole thing has gone too far. It's bad enough that we have abandoned the trial-and-error method and are teaching children about sex in school, that everyone is buying X-rated videotapes, that baseball players are on billboards and in magazines in their underwear (can you imagine Honus Wagner, Tris Speaker, or "Ducky" Medwick going public in their B.V.D.s?), and that daytime soaps have people who aren't even married to each other kissing with their mouths open and thrashing about in concupiscent abandon, but now gnomish grannies have taken to the airways saying things that Masters wouldn't even mention to Johnson.

Dr. Ruth is just another example of the current wave of explicitness that has robbed sex of all its mystery. I long for the bygone days when I was growing up in the mid-'50s and groups of us pimply pubescents would drive over to the Sears outlet in Carrollton to salivate over the corset section of the new Fall-Winter Catalog, or would get fiercely aroused by medical books featuring cross-sections of the human reproductive system.

We were told, and took it as an article of faith, that insanity would result from reading *National Geographic* before our librarian, Miss Martha Arnold, had drawn brassieres on the topless natives. Movies of the day had convinced us that no one used profanity, that all married people slept in twin beds, and that the logical consequence of kissing (done then with all four lips closed) was a fast fade to waves crashing on the beach at night. (Even though I am forty-eight years old, I still get excited going across the causeway to Jekyll Island.)

Another objection I have to Dr. Ruth is that she renders the sexually explicit so absolutely anti-erotic. It takes me back to the period of my youth when the most sexually explicit event of the year was the coming of one of two educational sex-dramas to the Palace Theater in Bowdon. The films, *Mom and Dad* and *Bob and Sally*, though educational in nature, were thought to be so sensational in content that separate showings were required for males and females and, as trumpeted in the previews for these coming attractions, both featured "a trained nurse in attendance throughout."

Sexual tension would build in Bowdon for weeks in anticipation of these epics, and grown men who hadn't been to the picture show since the advent of talkies would skulk in from the nether reaches of west Georgia and east Alabama to line up for the screenings.

The trained nurse always looked suspiciously like an off-duty waitress from a truck stop on the Bankhead Highway, complete with chipped nail polish and a hair net, and the only mildly titillating portion of the movie showed a fully dressed young couple thrashing about in the back of a 1948 Ford.

They were soon to learn that when lust overtakes reason, the inevitable result, aside from the crashing waves, is babies. All this, of course, was followed by wholesale shame and consternation.

As in the case with Dr. Ruth, the effect was decidedly anti-erotic. Now that I think of it, given a choice between Bob and Sally and Dr. Ruth, I would have to go for the movie. At least at the Palace you had a trained nurse in attendance and could get some Milk Duds. (April 1985)

DAILY CHECK OF THE OBITUARY PAGE SPURS A TRIP DOWN TELEVISION'S MEMORY LANE

Recognizing fully that nostalgia, like incontinence, is an affliction of old age, I must nonetheless confess to experiencing a wave of it (nostalgia, not incontinence) when I noted in the recent obituaries that the 1950s TV personality, Jerry Lester, had been permanently canceled.

I subscribe to S. J. Perelman's practice of getting up and turning immediately to the obituaries and, if I find I'm not included, planning the rest of my day. I was thus engaged some weeks past when I saw in the newspaper's roll call of the recently expired a short obituary chronicling the death of Jerry Lester at age 85. My fading memory swept me back to the early days of TV and the *Broadway Open House*, a vaudeville-style mix of music and jokes which ran on NBC in 1950 and 1951 that was hosted by

Jerry Lester. It is generally conceded to be the precursor of all network late night shows.

Lester was a typical Borscht Belt comedian who shared cohosting duties of the *Broadway Open House* with Morey Amsterdam, later to gain fame as a player on the *Dick Van Dyke Show*. Lester's overblown style involved gags delivered from the side of his mouth followed by rim shots from the drummer. He was an absolute master of eyebrow innuendo and, in that regard, while I remember Lester and Amsterdam vividly, the performer from the *Broadway Open House* who is etched most vividly in my memory is a zaftig blonde named Dagmar. (I am blessed with what doctors characterize as a "pornographic memory.") The stupefyingly constructed Dagmar achieved one-name fame long before Cher, Elvis, Madonna, or Kato.

In 1949, my father went deep into debt to buy one of Bowdon, Georgia's, first television sets, conferring instant celebrity status upon our family. It was an RCA cabinet model (with doors) which, at $450, had a higher value than all of the rest of our furniture put together. Neighbors would begin dropping in around 9 a.m. to watch the WSB-TV test pattern and, in good weather conditions, exclaim about its clarity. Programming was very limited, but the *Broadway Open House* was a definite 11 p.m. high point for me as Dagmar, in gowns so low that you couldn't tell if she was in them and trying to get out or out of them and trying to get back in, never failed to provoke adolescent spasms of heavy breathing and impure thought. She played the quintessential dumb blonde and her skirts were tight to the point that her short steps caused her to walk like an American tourist after a bad Mexican meal.

The marvelously voluptuous Dagmar had been signed on by Lester to deliver recitals of inane poetry in a wonderfully ingenious, deadpan manner. The poems were a secondary attraction to her bountiful balcony, and ultimately she stole so many scenes from Lester that he abandoned the series for greener pastures (or less competitive Tetons).

It's hard to imagine that all of these vivid black and white memories go back forty-five years, and that somber realization evokes the lines written in the movie *Network* by Patty Chayevsky for William Holden to the effect that, "One morning you wake up and realize for the first time that it's a hell of a lot closer to the end than it is to the beginning."

Indulging in nostalgia does indeed provoke the grim realization that the shadows are growing longer or, as that great American philosopher, Ralph Waldo Emerson (it was either Emerson or Pigmeat Markham; I always get those two mixed up), so succinctly put it, "Tempus sho do fugit." (April 1995)

TEENAGE ARGOT WILL BRING THE DECLINE AND FALL OF OUR NOBLE LANGUAGE

As I lounged lump-like and leaden by the steaming pool of a club in the northwest quadrant of the city, the babble of nonstop teen-age patter drifted through the torpid haze in an unending and ungrammatical stream. Treading the thin white line that separates heat stroke from hallucination, I wondered vaguely why America's youth—even the inmates of some of the city's most expensive schools—was so stunningly inarticulate.

Could it be the effect of long-term brain baking by years of powerful TV rays? Is there some toxic agent in Clearasil that somehow seeped into the teen-age cortex and stunted that portion responsible for comprehensible speech? Had decibel-deafening rock music and electric hair dryers forever numbed or fricasseed the faculties required for coherent communication?

Two north-side debs in my immediate earshot came upon one another after an apparent absence of a day or so and, after the obligatory shrieks of recognition and delight at this serendipitous reunion, lapsed into an argot that bordered on the untranslatable. I have long deplored and, on occasion, publicly decried the perverse tendency of today's youngsters to confuse the verb "to go" with the verb "to say," but after a few minutes of involuntary eavesdropping on these two bubble heads, my mind was literally screaming for even a trace of grammatical utterance.

"So she goes like, 'What do you mean Madonna got her hair cut?' and I go like, 'Really, I saw her in a video, and she's, like, trashed that grody old bra and has, like, really short hair.'"

Another phenomenon in the current speech pattern of the pimply people is a persistent and grating habit of responding to any declarative sentence with the word "really" as in:

Deb I: "Where have you been?"

Deb II: "Like, we visited my parents in Marietta."

Deb I: "Really."

The response is not intended to convey incredulity (though reacting to the above example, some might wonder that one would voluntarily confess to having kinfolks in Cobb County), nor is it an exclamation of approval (the word "neat" is used in those situations). Rather, it is simply a completely neutral verbal reflex indicating nothing more than "I understand."

In response to my minor poolside fulmination on this particular trend, my nineteen-year-old daughter, Nona, offered that it was nothing more than the modern day equivalent of "Is that so?" or "You don't say?" When I huffily observed that those phrases were never used in the South but were employed almost exclusively in the vapid reaches of the Midwest, my leathery spouse, who was lounging nearby in the manner of a languid lizard on a hot rock, dreamily revealed her humble origins by pointing out that the Southern equivalent of "really" was "do tell?"

Sensing that my outcries were falling on deaf and indifferent ears, I plunged back into my steamy reverie and wondered if prior to the time the Roman Empire slipped beneath the surface with a great sucking sound there had been a distant early warning in the form of a total breakdown in the speech patterns of their teenagers, for example:

"Like, Flavius, those games are like fixed. I mean, like, those lions are just pretending to eat those Christians."

"Really." (August 1986)

BETTER TO SHOUT THAN TO SHOOT

I hate to sound a note of caution when our president has struck such a marvelously resounding chord in the jingoistic loins of our angry and aroused nation. But, being fully aware that the opening battles of our Arabian adventure are going to be fought on *Nightline* and refereed by Ted Koppel, I have a genuine concern that is beginning to scab and fester (not to be confused with a group of Cobb County urologists by the same name).

I don't suggest for a minute that our troops can't overcome the Iraqi forces. I am fully convinced that the 101st Airborne Division could, if unleashed and unfettered, kick Saddam Hussein's behind so badly he would spend the rest of his life walking around on his elbows.

No, it's in the area of florid rhetoric that I believe the United States is experiencing a Bluster Gap.

In terms of threats, taunts, and gibes, the Iraqis are way ahead. At the drop of a fez, Saddam and his minions will spout rhetorical flourishes that absolutely take one's breath away in terms of their hyperbolic and vehement audacity. Before our troops could disembark (military for "get off the boat") in Saudi Arabia, Saddam and his coterie launched into flowery fulminations promising to "pluck out their eyes" or "spill rivers of blood that not even the sands of the great desert can absorb."

Watching his nightly monologue, one imagines a staff of sweaty writers sitting in the back of the tent coming up with curses like, "May a dyspeptic camel defile your Tupperware," or, "May Roseanne Barr sit on your Pop-Tarts."

Our leader, on the other hand, will preface his responses with "golly" or "gee," and then go on to give some nasal white-bread response that wouldn't intimidate a determined Avon lady. White House insiders confide that in private his responses are significantly more salty, ranging from, "Oh, yeah?" to "Who says so?" or, when he is particularly incensed, "Your mother!"

It seems to me we are in serious danger of losing the battle of bluster, and my advice is to immediately create a new cabinet-level position for a Secretary of Imprecations, whose sole duty would be to appear on the news and answer Saddam's rantings measure for measure.

We need look no further than the ranks of our ever-choleric TV wrestlers to find our man. All the president has to do is flip on Channel 47 and World Wrestling Federation to find someone who can give Saddam the old what for.

My personal choice for the position would be Hulk Hogan. Hogan, a maniacal-looking taxpayer with a perpetual tan and greasy dancing pectorals, is in an ongoing shouting match with a bearded behemoth called simply "Earthquake" (though that could be a nickname) as they bait each other over the upcoming and eagerly awaited "Summer Slam."

It is a wondrous and sometimes frightening moment when the fulminating mastodons stand nose to nose and shout threats filled with passion, imagination, and a fair amount of spittle at each other, while the announcer tries his best to look serious and ponder the cosmic implications of who will take the Zircon-encrusted heavyweight belt from whom.

While President Bush and the 101st Airborne Division will certainly do the job if and when the Summer Slam in Saudi starts in earnest, I think that in the meantime we can agree it's better to be shouting than shooting and that we need to have Hulk Hogan up front if we really expect anyone to read our lips. (August 1990)

A NEW GENDER GAP: ONE MAN'S TALE ON CHILI NIGHT

There are sociologists, researchers at large universities, radio talk show hosts, and ultra-liberal columnists who are forever squeaking and braying to the effect that there are no gender-based differences when it comes to a person's capacity for compassion in a crisis situation.

All this proves to me is that no sociologists, researchers at large universities, radio talk show hosts, or ultra-liberal columnists have ever been attended by my wife during the course of a grizzly illness. The compassion contrast between the genders in my particular case study was made even more pointed by the fact that my own illness was preceded by a minor bout that my wiry wife engaged in with the same malaise.

One Saturday afternoon as I was busy watching professional bowling on television (there would appear to be some sort of league rule that each bowler's last name end with a vowel, preferably "i"), I was interrupted by my wife's thin, reedy voice saying, "I think I'm going to be sick."

As her indisposition had brought her in from an afternoon of cleaning the gutters, I instinctively sensed that it was a serious malady that would require loving care and devoted attention by me. I immediately leaped into action by sitting up on the sofa and suggesting that she should quit cleaning the gutters, put off ironing my shirts until the following day, and go upstairs and take her temperature, adding that as she was going to have to wait around for three or four minutes with a thermometer in her mouth, she might take that opportunity to make me a tuna fish sandwich with sweet pickles and lots of mayonnaise.

At this point her eyes turned completely white, both cheeks extended to their fullest limits and she bolted from the room with a stricken look.

As soon as possible (I think it was during the half-time ceremonies of a football game I had switched to), I rushed up to our bedroom to attend her, insisting again that she wait until the following day before getting around a hot iron.

I really don't think her episode was quite as severe as mine because in only one day she was, owing to my ministrations and the fact that she lounged around in bed for twenty-four hours, fully restored, an apple-cheeked, chirping picture of health.

Several evenings later, I came home for supper to find her stirring up a large cauldron of low-fat chili that was made from a recipe she found in a book called *The T-Factor Diet*. It allegedly contained only one fat gram per serving and was made with kidney beans soaked in chicken broth, chili powder, and used truck tire treads, which can be found on the side of any interstate highway. Except for the taste and the fact that it had the bouquet of a drag race, you'd have sworn it was the real thing.

To her credit, my wizened bride has never been a nag about my weight, but when she learned from my gabby secretary that I had caused my office chair to be let out, she began to bustle around officiously promoting diets that let you eat "all you want to eat" as long as you eat bean sprouts, yogurt, and plankton flown in daily from Lake Burton.

Although I ate only enough of the chili concoction to show my appreciation, I immediately fell desperately ill (studies at the Center for Communicable Disease have shown that the rankest form of salmonella thrives in a fat-free environment).

I quickly curled up on the main sofa in as close to the fetal position as my girth would allow, covered myself with a gathering of throws, and began to shiver and moan uncontrollably, pausing only for intermittent trips to the lavatory to "speak on the big white phone." One would imagine that this would provoke no end of tender attentions and expressions of concern from my spouse of long standing. One could hardly be more incorrect.

Standing over me with arms akimbo, she declared, "It's that thing I had. There's nothing you can do but tough it out."

Throughout my whole ordeal, she callously refused to administer any medication. This despite the fact that, as a one-sixteenth Creek Indian, she is in possession of a veritable treasure-trove of nostrums involving dried frog viscera, roots, ground berries, and scrapings from the walls of her microwave oven.

While because of my raging fever-induced delirium I cannot be quite sure, I believe I heard her talking on the phone to a friend, and though I was in and out of consciousness, I am reasonably certain I heard her say that I thought I was in a "mordibund" state. This followed by snorting gales of laughter and what sounded to me like the phrase, "a real wussy."

As I say, I can't vouch for this last part because of my fevered state, but I gladly offer this incomplete study to any serious researchers who are looking into the compassion gender gap, which I am convinced has engulfed our modern society.

If the researchers are not interested in my studies, I'd be more than glad to offer them the rest of the chili. (December 1990)

THE ULTIMATE OFFENSE: A BOOK-SELLING PLOY

As I sat in the green room of a local television station awaiting an opportunity to go on the air to flog my latest book (*The Sass Menagerie*, available at fine bookstores everywhere, or, for orders of two or more, I'll come out to your house, apartment, or double-wide and sign anything in that sucker you want), it occurred to me that there must be a better way to spur book sales than this approach.

I was even more firmly convinced when I only had a two-minute sliver of time and was followed by a ferret from the Atlanta zoo that got five minutes even though he couldn't talk. When I testily made this observation to the anchorman after the show, he said, "That's why the ferret got more time."

Driving back to the office from the interview, a sudden surge of blood reached my brain and the ultimate solution to hyping book sales occurred to me with blinding clarity. That is, of course, to get the Ayatollah Khomeini to publicly condemn the book and threaten my life or, preferably, the lives of my publishers, Simon & Lipschutz (New York, Philadelphia, and Austell). Why hadn't I thought of that in the first place?

When the Great One, in his role as Exalted Literary Critic, hurled bans at *The Satanic Verses* by Salman Rushdie, sales went off the charts. There was, of course, a dark side to the publicity in that the ayatollah offered $5.2 million to anyone who would send Mr. Rushdie to that great Autograph Party in the Sky. I confess right up front that I would be a little intimidated about this aspect of the program, but for a rush in book sales, I would be willing to have my wife start my car every morning for a year or so.

Attempting to put that pale thought to vivid action, I called long-distance information and attempted to get the telephone number of the ayatollah. Unfortunately, he had an unlisted tent and could not be reached. It probably was just as well because, searching my brain for anything in my last collection that might have the happy effect of giving offense to the Most Worthy One, I could recall only one blurb from a distant column to the effect that every time I saw him on television I thought he was Gabby Hayes in drag.

Realizing deep down that this flip and off-the-cuff observation wouldn't generate an Iranian bounty of more than $2,000 or $3,000, I began my quest for a condemnation by some other potentially indignant past victim of my venomous pen.

I called Roger Sund, the executive director of the Cobb County Chamber of Commerce, and pointed out that in one essay I had alleged that Cobb County was not as sophisticated as it held itself out to be, going on to report that a group of anthropologists at the University of Georgia recently had discovered a tribe of people living in the woods in south Cobb County who still worship the Big Chicken.

I suggested to him that the chamber might want to put out a contract on me and offered to kick in a couple of hundred bucks to the fund myself if he could get some radio and TV time to publicize the threat. Mr. Sund said that he was not interested, in that the chamber already had relocated all the Big Chicken worshipers in mobile homes near Smyrna and, "Besides," he said, "nobody in Cobb County reads your stuff anyway."

Undaunted, I resumed poring over my prior literary output for other serious slights that could be thumped into a newsworthy public grievance with resulting salutary effects on book sales.

I had observed irreverently in the past that if Ronald Reagan had one more face lift, his navel was going to pop up over his shirt collar. But, on reflection, I decided a death threat from an ex-president would not even be sufficiently newsworthy to get a blurb in *Creative Loafing.*

I then recalled that I had once publicly suggested that Six Flags Over Georgia install a new thriller and death-defying attraction consisting of an automobile ride with Hosea Williams (talk about your Scream Machine). Remembering that Mr. Williams was pretty volatile and, according to recent newspaper accounts, armed to the teeth, I called his office to see if he might utter a threat with respect to my book but through his secretary was given a polite brushoff: "Tell that chump I ain't studying him."

If any readers have any suggestions as to how I might have given or could in the future give ultimate offense to some powerful and newsworthy person and provoke a public jihad along the line of *The Satanic Verses* hurrah, I would welcome their suggestions. In the meantime, I am optimistically storing provisions in a secret hiding place against the possibility that I might have to go underground for a spell if I ever come up with the right person to antagonize. (February 1989)

JUST WHAT DOES "HAMMACHER SCHLEMMER" MEAN IN GERMAN?

I wish the activist legions would give a rest to reproduction, fur-wearing, and the greenhouse effect and turn their guns on mail-order catalogs before it's too late.

In olden days, when a person did something that identified them as an easy mark capable of being thoroughly mulcted, travelling gypsies would place some sort of secret mark over the door of the unsuspecting pigeon and thereafter hordes of their colleagues would flock by to take advantage of the dupe thus designated.

Nowadays, the same result is achieved when you buy something from a mail-order catalog. Once this happens, the catalog company sends your name and address to a huge underground silo in Junk Mail, Idaho, where it is placed on a master list. Thereafter your mailman risks a double hernia daily delivering towering stacks of ever proliferating mail-order catalogs, most of them trumpeting an incredible array of worthless goods.

In a recent barrage, I was struck by a catalog that proved beyond any doubt the low opinion mail-order companies have for their unseen customers. It was from an outfit called Hammacher Schlemmer and offered an astounding assortment of useless items for shoppers who are too lazy to forge through the teeming malls themselves or who are candidates for the South Georgia Home for the Profligate Rich.

Although I didn't know what *Hammacher Schlemmer* meant, I had been introduced to the company about twenty-five years ago while in New York City on legal business with a former acquaintance, Richard A. Allison (not his real name), who was known to be a card-carrying member of the idle rich.

Mr. Allison, though a native of the Hookworm and Pellagra Belt in Southwest Alabama, was born with a silver spoon in his mouth. (Aside from a slight speech impediment and excessive drooling when agitated, the plucky Mr. Allison managed to overcome this handicap.) He was always quick to point out that he had attended Princeton, and while I don't have anything against Ivy Leaguers, they do have an unfortunate tendency to speak as though they are dictating to a stonecutter and will often say things like, "Be that as it may…."

As we roamed the city, Mr. Allison insisted in his patronizing way that we go by Hammacher Schlemmer so he could get some "great and unusual gift" for his father. I can't remember what he bought him (the options I still recall were tungsten socks, vibrating underwear, a foot-operated fish scaler, and a hand-carried portable toilet), but I do remember being left with the overall impression that this establishment was clearly a place for people with more money than critical judgment.

In reviewing their current catalog, I discovered that in the intervening twenty-five years, nothing much had changed at Hammacher Schlemmer.

For the affluent Mafioso, the catalog offers a remote-control car starter that also "activates your car's headlights and sounds a locating whistle allowing you to find your car in a crowded parking lot."

Other "must have" items included a "snore-reducing pillow" that, from the look of it, would be most effective when held tightly over the snorer's face for five or ten minutes, an orthopedic pet bed (for those who may be reluctant to take their animals to a chiropractor), a battery-operated nose and ear hair trimmer (guaranteed to cause even the most jaded dinner companion to sit up and take notice), moisture-absorbing chamois socks, a hands-free snowball maker, and a solar-ventilated golf cap with a built-in fan for the forehead (for those seeking to establish themselves as the ultimate dork).

In the section modestly titled "The Future Now," Hammacher Schlemmer features a vacuum-powered insect-disposal system that "lets you quickly capture and dispose of insects at a comfortable distance without requiring direct contact or leaving any mess." This causes me to believe that the old-fashioned fly swatter will soon go the way of the buggy whip for all who can afford the modestly priced ($49.95, with six disposable cartridges at an additional $29.95) vacuum.

Finally, they offer an ultrasonic dog repeller that "produces a high-frequency sound wave that will deter bothersome or attacking dogs." If their research department can ever perfect this item so it can be used against insurance agents and telephone solicitors, I think they may be on to something.

Provided an exception can be carved out for the tastefully designed and beautifully presented catalog titled "Victoria's Secret," I would favor immediate legislation requiring criminal sanctions for the distribution or possession of mail-order catalogs.

And, for those of you who are getting up to call or write your legislator, you can tell them I have made diligent inquiry and have learned that *Hammacher Schlemmer* is German for "there's one born every minute." (February 1990)

OBESE ABUSE (OR, FAT PEOPLE NEED LOVE TOO)

With all this talk about battered women, I'd like to know if anyone is interested in or trying to prevent an equally serious and even more widespread problem—obese abuse. While I certainly agree that it is reprehensible for any husband to roll his wife in eggs, milk, and bread crumbs, I feel just as strongly that there is a need for increased concern and perhaps even legislative action in the area of caustic remarks by wives (or husbands) regarding weight control problems of their spouses.

At a recent cocktail gathering, an unknown but very comely lady approached me and said, "You remind me of Erma Bombeck a little." Before I could respond, my wife replied, "If you saw him in a bathing suit he'd remind you of her a lot." This, I submit, is the kind of loutish and insensitive remark one might expect from someone who feels "stuffed" after a half piece of toast.

I will concede that Erma and I are both what Jane Russell calls "full-figured," but still, despite my previously acknowledged tendency to "bunch up" when sitting down, we are, I think, most pleasant in appearance.

I have long since made a separate peace with my weight problem by coming to the mature judgment that if you can't be effective, you can at least be philosophic. I thought it a significant breakthrough when at age forty I made a firm resolution to no longer continuously hold my breath on the beach. A second breakthrough was my decision to quit reading the myriad diets that appear so relentlessly in every magazine from *Redbook* to *Dragstrip Journal*. After forty years I finally realized they were all fads, mostly ridiculous and completely ineffective, and that you could go blindfolded to any magazine counter and pick up something along the following lines:

The All-You-Can-Eat Diets—These permit you to eat all you want provided you limit your selection to squash and guavas.

Dr. Stillman's Water Diet—Completely ineffective and produces a noticeably bad side effect…"audible sloshing."

Dr. Hosea Williams' Driving School and Weight Control Clinic—Just another "crash" diet.

The Orson Welles/Paul Masson Diet—You can trust Paul to sell no wine before its time, but it would be a grave error in judgment to leave Orson alone for even a moment with your groceries.

The Eat-Only-When-Standing-Up Diet—This breakthrough promised that you would "startle your friends" with rapid weight loss. I tried the diet for a week and the only person I startled was the maître d' at Nikolai's Roof.

I've also found that if one follows a few commonsense rules there will be less preoccupation with a weight problem. For example, an overweight person is much less conspicuous while wearing a bathrobe, except, of course, at wedding receptions, business lunches, etc. In addition, one should avoid buying clothes at trendy shops like Britches which, if they carry your size at all, characterize it as the "Porker" or "Chubbette" model.

Instead, trade with establishments which euphemistically term suits shaped like Hefty Bags as their "Executive Cut."

I would also caution against weighing on any scales in a doctor's office. They are always high. My surly spouse (Have you ever noticed that thin people are rarely jolly?) suggested that my scales might be as high as those in the doctor's office if I ever let go of the towel rack while weighing. I thought it just as well not to let her know that the last time I tried that maneuver the digital readout on my scales flashed "One at a time, please."

In summary, my advice is not to worry about weight controls unless there is clear and present danger of terminal obesity. In that connection, I have prepared and am willing to share "Dr. Steed's Seven Danger Signals for Terminal Obesity." They are:

1. Being ordered off a public beach for having no top to your bathing suit.
2. Chrome on refrigerator handle shows noticeable wear.
3. Dirt accumulates in rings around your neck during summer months.
4. Angle of necktie exceeds forty-five degrees beyond vertical.
5. Hallucinations about being followed by the chicken in "Smilin' Jack."
6. Wife needs seat belt or Velcro fasteners on sheets and pajamas to keep from rolling to your side of bed.
7. Sudden disappearance of feet.

Unless at least four of the seven signals appear, thin spouses should be required to keep their counsel and their more ample mates should strive to maintain a sense of humor about the whole business. My hero in this regard is the beautiful, bubbly, and bountiful opera star Beverly Sills, who, having agreed to make a Western movie, insisted on a clause in her contract to the effect that if the script called for her to ride off into the sunset, the producers were required to find a horse whose behind was bigger than hers. I'd ride off with Erma or Beverly. Anytime. (November 1980)

BEWARE OF THOSE JOCKEY SHORTS

During the course of the recent political unpleasantness, I was struck by just how often officeholders and officeholder wannabes served up bits of folk wisdom allegedly learned at the knee of their mother/father/grandparent/professor/family proctologist, etc.

The campaign seemed to be marked by a sustained spasm of self-serving shibboleth spouting such as, "My grandmother always told me an incumbent should never agree to a debate with an underdog." Or, "As my late Daddy used to say, 'An incumbent's tax returns are nobody else's damn business.'" If the relative proffering the helpful bromide was both dead and of some ethnic persuasion, it seemed to invest the quote with even deeper meaning, as in, "I don't care what the press thinks, the girl said she was eighteen and, like my late Armenian grandmother used to say, 'The dogs bark, but the caravan moves on.'" (Politicians will often end a sentence with both a preposition and a cliché.)

Over the course of the campaign, I became grimly aware of the fact that my parents, grandparents, et al., had been dismally derelict in failing to pass along to me any wise and apt aphorisms with which I could pepper my conversation and pass on to my progeny.

In dredging back over a lifetime of memories, I could recall only one tidbit imparted by my late father. In 1954, as he was putting me on a Greyhound bus bound from Bowdon to Macon for my first year of college, he looked me square in the eye, grasped my arm with his big calloused hand, and said, "Don't let those folks at Mercer make you room with anyone who wears them brief-type jockey shorts." I never fully understood what he meant by that advice, but it's been a code I've always tried to live by.

In any case, I felt my inventory of sage sayings woefully barren and bereft of bromides. Even more sobering was the realization that I had no database of meaningful maxims to pass along to my own children, who doubtless have been pecking through my conversational droppings for years in search of some illuminating kernels of wisdom.

This bleak thought was so troubling that I resolved to remedy the situation and, setting my chin as firmly as my ample wattles would permit, I racked my mind and memory for pithy epigrams to pass along to my eager offspring.

My exertions were rewarded, and after only a few days, I had already begun to compile a worthy repertoire. I see myself in a cardigan sweater and slippers smoking a pipe full of Taster's Choice, while sitting before a knot of rapt grandchildren and sharing a few of the following wisdom-encrusted gems:

- Unless you want to smell like the Gabor sisters, avoid shaking hands with men who wear those musk-laden colognes.
- Don't stand near a microwave oven if you're wearing a truss.
- Never pick up a hitchhiker wearing nothing but a cowboy hat and a hospital gown.
- Nobody's life is completely worthless; you can always serve as a bad example.

This is, admittedly, just a small beginning but, as my late Latvian great-grandmother used to say, "Bubba, Disney World wasn't built in a day." (January 1995)

CABLE TV LETS THE VANDALS IN THE LIVING ROOM

For some time now I have become increasingly convinced that the most pernicious threat to our Western civilization lies not in the Red Menace, pit bulls, school prayer, the environmentally hostile "greenhouse effect," or even the deadly grammatical patterns of our youngsters. Rather, it is the persistent and poisonous mind pollutant pumped directly and relentlessly into our homes in the form of cable television.

While other less concerned citizens choose to ignore this threat and follow their own trivial pursuits, I, in sporadic fits of patriotic fervor, dive into my humpback leather couch at intervals and, like Jacques Cousteau, probe the murky electronic depths of cable television, surfacing occasionally to sound an alarm that, doubtless, will go unnoticed and unappreciated. But then, everyone thought Geraldo Rivera was crazy, too.

As noted in my earlier dispatches, I am something of a virtuoso on the remote-control keyboard. With deft, lightning-like strokes, I can do a fly pattern through sixty-plus channels of pap and drivel (not to be confused with the large Atlanta advertising firm of the same name) and thus keep a jaundiced eye on all the troublesome activity infesting our electronic subconscious.

Probably the most distressing recent development on cable television is the advent of TV fishing. There are actually people in our society who are watching two bozos in a bateau bobbing about in some Godforsaken backwater fishing. The dialogue goes something like this:

Play-by-play angler: "Boy howdy, that's a big 'un!"

Color angler: "That *is* a big 'un."

Whereupon they reel in a carp for a cameo appearance, hoist it for the camera, and then, for reasons I have not been able to fathom, release it. What chance does our civilization have for the long haul when we know that there are grown people who, presumably, are licensed to drive automobiles and are doubtless producing children, who sit for long intervals watching other people catch fish and turn them loose day after day?

Another ominous development is telemarketing. One fascinating program emanating from (where else?) California features a beefy pitchman who, at first blush, seems to be auctioning off a variety of remaindered goods to a crowd that looks as though they would gather to see a root canal. The crowd keeps bidding the merchandise higher and higher, which causes a skinny stooge to the right of the auctioneer to get so excited that he begins to whirl on his axis like a demented dervish approaching a state of huckster rhapsody.

Finally, when the schlock merchandise has been bid up to a point where the auctioneer dare not risk exciting his sidekick further, he does not, as one might suspect, sell it to the highest bidder. No, he announces that the unbelievable merchandise (brass hat-racks, zircon-incrusted gold unisex neck chains, horse statues with clocks in their stomach and the like) will not sell for $65 as bid but will go for $19.95 to all those who will "get up and call in now."

But this is just one of the ways to affect a transfer of funds to TV performers from the eager and easily mulcted souls who so avidly follow their electronic antics. Witness the continued fiscal success of the swarm of "televangelists," which *Time* magazine featured in a recent cover story on the burgeoning phenomenon.

My personal pick from the preachers now swarming the airways are the Bakkers, Jim and Tammie Faye, who are forever bobbing about in a sea of fiscal crisis but, just when they have convinced you that their ship is about to slip beneath the surface with a great sucking sound, the faithful respond with shekels enough to float it even higher. Tammie Faye seems to apply her makeup with a trowel (I live in fear that someday she will be found slumped in a doorway, overdosed on a bad batch of Maybelline), and the Rev. Jim, with the love offerings of the faithful, has just completed what may well be the largest water slide in Christendom. All summer long he appeared on the airwaves looking like a forlorn chipmunk in a yellow hard hat importuning his TV parishioners to send in more money to complete the water slide. I had visions of one of his flock swooshing down the towering monster, flying off its unfinished end, and landing with a deadly thump in Beulah Land. Happily, the project was completed during the summer, and the Bakkers now offer, in addition to traditional spiritual succor, a kind of Six Flags Over Heaven in Fort Mill, South Carolina.

Rapid clicking of the remote-control buttons reveals a phantasmagoria of faces that include Regis Philbin, Dr. Ruth, the ever-lachrymose Sally Struthers, a meat house of wrestlers shouting imprecations into the camera, and a cooking show featuring a bagged-out creole in red suspenders who keeps saying, "I garroon-tee" for "guarantee." This stuff, I'm sure, is turning our brains into that old-fashioned peanut butter with the oil slick on top, and my guess is that there is some central sinister force behind it all. Stay tuned. (January 1987)

HAS PROGRESS COME TO ALABAMA? ASK THE FELLOW WITH A PHONE IN HIS GRAVE

My ancestral home, Bowdon, Georgia, is sixty miles due west of Atlanta and it is, as my brother Michael, who still lives there, often says, "dangerously close to Alabama."

It is sometimes forgotten that Georgia once owned all of what is now Alabama but in 1786 sold it to the Talladega Indians for a case of pocket mirrors, one hundred pounds of salt, and a jeweled truss. Historians, then and now, have observed that Georgia got the better end of the bargain. In my youth, we West Georgians always appreciated Alabama as it gave us something to look down on and, even though there was no marker delineating the state line, we knew when we began to see rusted car carcasses upon cinder blocks, rotting mattresses in the front yard, and wringer-type washing machines on the front stoop, we had passed out of Georgia and into Darkest Alabama. Because Alabama's state bird is Conway Twitty and the state motto is "Nobody's life is completely worthless; you can always serve as a bad example," its citizens necessarily expect to endure some measure of obloquy from their neighbors from time to time.

However, in recent years, I have been under the impression that progress had been made in Alabama, and that its country ways and aberrant behavior patterns were gradually being replaced by a new level of sophistication as evidenced by significant declines in the sale of polyester garments, fewer truck-tire-lined driveways, and a shrinking number of tree trunks painted white, etc.

Alas, I was living in a fool's paradise (not to be confused with Demopolis, which has that phrase emblazoned on its police cars and public signage as a city motto). My awakening came in the form of a report from my brother Mike that a man in Alabama had been buried recently with his portable telephone, thus reviving all of my darkest suspicions about the lack of sophistication in Alabama and, at the same time, putting new meaning in the term "call waiting." (It brings to mind the words of the classic country song, "If my telephone ain't ringing, I assume it still ain't you.")

It is rarely productive to inquire into the logic of anything that goes on in Alabama, but one does wonder why one of its citizens would be interred with a portable telephone. A number of questions come to mind:

(1) Did his relatives realize he would have to call quickly before the batteries ran out?

(2) Did they keep paying the telephone company for the service and, if so, for how long?

(3) Did they anticipate that they might need to get in touch with the departed at some later date? ("Lamar Eugene, where's the weed-eater at?")

Maybe they were thinking of the old 1930s gospel song which begins, "Operator, information, get me Jesus on the line," but one would think that if the deceased had led a life of rectitude and righteousness, he would not need a touch-tone telephone to communicate with his Maker.

And, in connection with communications between Alabamians and their Maker (I'm not called the master of segue for nothing), there is a little known but true story about the last words of Jesus to the tribes then wandering in Alabama as he was about to leave this mortal coil. He is said to have told them, "Act dumb till I return." The tribes, as evidenced most recently by the telephone in the crypt, have been ever faithful. (January 1996)

IF JOGGERS NEED HEAVIER HANDS, WHY DON'T THEY CARRY BRICKS?

For those countless readers who look to me as a distant early-warning system in the area of unwholesome trends, fetishes, and aberrations in the social order, I am sorry to have to report that jogging, that persistent combination of masochism and exhibitionism, appears to be on the brink of giving birth to yet another sub-fad.

On Sunday last, as I was weaving my automobile through the never-ending stream of sweaty joggers on Howell Mill Road on my way to obtain a nutritious sausage biscuit with cheese, I was jolted from my customary torpor by my wife's shrill exclamation, "Look at all those dumbbells!"

"It's just the usual spasm of Sunday-morning joggers," I replied, trying to concentrate on my maneuvering and the sausage biscuit with cheese looming ever larger in my mind's eye.

"No," she said, "I'm talking about those things they're carrying in their hands while they run." Closer inspection revealed that my wizened companion was correct. About every fourth jogger seemed to be carrying what appeared to be an oversized pair of brass knuckles in each hand as they huffed and lurched through the public streets. (While we are on that subject, I think some legislation ought to be introduced requiring joggers to pursue their unsightly compulsion in places other than public thoroughfares. With the exception of drag racing and stealing hubcaps, I know of no other human pastime so monumentally arrogant that it presumes to preempt the public roads and byways to its own ends.)

Subsequent inquiry on my part revealed that the odd-looking devices being carried about by the joggers were specially configured weights called "Heavy Hands." In fact, some clinical material for further research surfaced in the person of my son Joshua, who revealed that he had invested in a pair of Heavy Hands, though he was unable to give me a satisfactory explanation as to their actual purpose.

Those who have been watching this sweaty social phenomenon develop over the years will quickly observe that there need be no requirement for a valid purpose to create a jogging sub-fad. These poor souls whose brains have been systematically cauliflowered through years of sustained jogging have no capacity to resist the outrageous accoutrements relentlessly foisted on them by unscrupulous hucksters.

Consider, for example, the terry cloth elastic bands that joggers wrap about their heads and wrists; the specially designed jogging shoes themselves, each generation uglier than its predecessor and all of which resemble Hush Puppies with birth defects; the little radios with headsets to render joggers even more oblivious to oncoming traffic; the gym shorts worn, inexplicably, over and outside sweat pants; the atrocious velour pajama-type outfits with racing stripes that increasing numbers of non-joggers have taken to wearing to shopping malls, grocery stores, and picture shows; etc.

This latest fad began to take on sinister implications the more I pondered it. What, for example, had happened to the famous "Bird Man" who jogged along flapping his arms up and down in the manner of a gooney bird making an unscheduled landing? There had been no reported sightings of him for months. Had he perhaps become a victim of Heavy Hands?

Why, assuming there was some utilitarian purpose to be achieved by darting about in the public streets with these ridiculous appendages, couldn't the same result be achieved through the simple expedient of carrying a brick in each hand? (In fact, many bricks have mysterious holes in them which could well be adapted to just this end.) Were the items designed and are they in fact being used as corrective devices for joggers with limp wrists? All of these seem to be questions worthy of broader inquiry and, while I have no answers at this point, I commend them to other interested parties for closer consideration.

I offer all this at some considerable personal risk for, as my wife so frequently points out, I have established a reputation (because of previous courageous public utterings) for being anti-physical fitness. While it is true that I once characterized the Peachtree Road Race as resembling "a stampede which would convince the unknowing that some sinister force had flushed everyone out of Marietta in their underwear and was herding them south with electric cattle prods," and while I did have a cow-catcher welded to the front of my automobiles as a light-hearted protest against the ever-increasing number of joggers who clot the public streets and steadfastly refuse to yield the right of way to those who presume to use them for purposes as mundane as going back and forth to work or, on weekends, to fetch sausage biscuits with cheese, there is absolutely no basis to the widely held notion that I am anti-physical fitness. That proposition, I submit, is ridiculous on its face. After all, you're not born with a body like this. You have to work at it every day. (July 1985)

JUDGE WAPNER: THE PEOPLE'S JUSTICE

I hate to sound like one of the old codgers sitting around some cafeteria or Howard Johnson's after gumming down another meal who, with a fresh squirt of blood to the brain, will start ruminating about "What is the world coming to?" However, having filed that disclaimer, I must admit to some disquiet when I read in the newspapers that in a recent poll more Americans recognized Judge Joseph A. Wapner of TV's *The People's Court* than any justice of the U.S. Supreme Court. Even more shocking, many could not name a single justice on the Supreme Court.

By the sheerest of coincidences, just a few days after my sluggish consciousness had been further numbed by this appalling intelligence, I was invited by a friend at WSB-TV, the lively and zaftig Anna Ornduff, to have lunch with the good Judge Wapner, who was coming to town to flog his ultra-successful TV program. Notwithstanding the fact that the name of the program always had sounded to me like some communist star chamber, it is a phenomenon of the first order having been featured on the front page of *The Wall Street Journal*, in the *New Yorker*, on *20/20*, and in almost every major newspaper in the Western world.

As I was keen to meet Judge Wapner in person, I accepted the WSB offer with alacrity (unfortunately, Alacrity had a conflicting engagement and couldn't make it to lunch with Hizzoner, settling out of court for an autographed napkin).

The chief reason for my acute interest in meeting Judge Wapner was to investigate a suspicion I had long harbored that the judge was really Ted Mack of the old *Original Amateur Hour*, who mysteriously disappeared in the early 1960s when TV executives belatedly concluded that the American public was growing weary of CPAs playing "The Flight of the Bumble-Bee" on a bicycle pump. When I first saw *The People's Court*, I was convinced that the producers had recycled the benign and nasal Mr. Mack into a small claims judge for purposes of television.

At our luncheon the good-natured Judge Wapner responded without rancor to my gimlet-eyed inquiry by disclaiming any relation to Mr. Mack and produced a California driver's license and discharge papers to support his denial.

Thus assuaged, I dived into my lobster and corn chowder and resumed my furtive sidelong glances at Ms. Ornduff's impressive balcony, while thoroughly enjoying my visit with the handsome and genial Judge Joseph A. Wapner. I learned he was a real jurist who, in a pre-TV incarnation, served as presiding judge of the Los Angeles Superior Court, the largest court in the United States. The judge and his lively and lovely wife of forty-two years, Mickey, were so charming that I even resolved that if I assayed to write about him I would forswear any rude or flip comment like, for example, comparisons to Ted Mack of the *Original Amateur Hour*.

I also vowed to begin watching his program and, having put that pale thought to vivid action a couple of evenings in a row, found it to be thoroughly enjoyable as the earnest, stern, and sometimes peckish Judge Wapner dispensed small claims justice in a fair but summary fashion.

A typical case, titled "Bye Bye Basketballs," dealt with a backyard brouhaha involving two steaming litigants who barely spoke English. The plaintiff, a gnomish woman of middle years and uncertain national origin, was suing to recover three basketballs that her son had accidentally caused to land in the yard of a horribly truculent neighbor who heatedly explained to Judge Wapner in what I took to be an obscure Serbo-Croatian dialect why she refused to return them—"I'm sick wid dis beesketboll. I had flu wid fever and got so nervous I had to go for my stomach to de doctor."

The judge, with Solomon-like wisdom, ordered the basketballs returned and adjured the parties to work out their differences, pointing out to the flared-nostril and nettled neighbor that it was easier to give back the balls than to come to court at frequent intervals. She seemed unrepentant to me, and I suspect that her yard remains a Bermuda Triangle for errant basketballs, notwithstanding the judge's wise and earnest counsel.

An interesting and regular post-verdict feature of each show is a debriefing of the litigants by a prissy looking court hanger-on named Doug Llewelyn. His interviews give the winners a chance to make sanctimonious noises about vindication while the losers' noses are rubbed in it with questions reminiscent of the famous, "Aside from that, Mrs. Lincoln, how did you enjoy the play?" From all appearances, Mr. Llewelyn then disappears offstage to suck lemons and tease his hair.

This brings us back (and, you must be thinking, not a moment too soon) to what steps can be taken by the Supreme Court to enhance its lackluster public image. My suggestion is that the justices could reconsider their ban on televised arguments or they could urge President Bush to nominate Judge Wapner for the next seat that becomes vacant. Even if he doesn't get confirmed, it would give the FBI a chance to clear up those Ted Mack rumors once and for all. (July 1989)

BEWARE OF WIVES BEARING GIFTS

It is difficult, painful, and almost impossible to believe that twenty-five years ago my apprehensive parents gave my hand in matrimony to the swarthy, suspect, and sexually precocious Linda Ruth McElroy in a simple but tasteful double ring ceremony in the Bowdon Methodist Church. Polite society in West Georgia was, in a word, aghast. Not since Edward VIII renounced the throne to marry the American commoner, Wallis Simpson, had there been such an egregious mismatch across social and class boundaries.

In the traditional engagement story reported dutifully by the society editor of the *Bowdon Bulletin*, the anxious mother of the bride-to-be, obviously grateful at the prospect that the fortuitous match might spare her dark and enigmatic daughter from an otherwise certain life of selling scuppernongs from the back of a pickup truck or reading palms in a dingy trailer, replied to a reporter's question as to when the nuptials would take place by blurting, "There'll be no nuptials until after the wedding!"

Through the many intervening years the social, class, and intellectual differences have grown more, rather than less, acute, and recurring questions repeated by one and all are, "What does he see in her? Why are they together?" Certainly elements of habit, inertia, lust, nostalgia, a long-standing dread of alimony, and the stark possibility of being awarded custody of the children all play a part in the inexplicable but remarkably durable union. Another unusual but very honest answer is that I simply could not bear the thought of not being around to see what absolutely absurd and useless gift the next wedding anniversary will bring.

Over the years my sinewy spouse, long suspected as the spiritual founder of a group of dedicated and perverse buyers whose motto is "When the going gets tough, the tough go shopping," has come up with a succession of anniversary presents, almost any of which, if introduced in evidence in a divorce proceeding, would cause the jury to find for me without leaving the box.

I'll admit that almost any wife, if subjected to the proper marketing techniques, will be guilty from time to time of buying her husband something ridiculous as evidenced by the continued sale of items such as lime-scented shaving cream. Certainly no grown man would purchase for himself a product which causes him to stand bleary-eyed before his sink in the predawn hours knowing that he is going into the long day smelling like a gin and tonic. My spouse, however, has a flair for selecting anniversary offerings which transcend the traditional boundaries of taste, practicality, utility, or cost.

Time and the pain of particular memories won't permit me to recount all of her bizarre anniversary gifts over the past quarter century, but if giving a few selected examples should, by happy chance, save just one person from wandering into a bad marriage, then this effort will not have been in vain. To that end, I submit the following:

A pair of genuine leather jeans which resulted in a case of diaper rash so severe that it steadfastly resisted a variety of industrial-strength unguents and ultimately caused my being featured as foldout in a little known but highly respected medical journal.

A copper quill holder which, doubtless because of technological advancements in the area of writing implements during the industrial revolution, came without quills.

A clear-plastic shower curtain permitting me the unhappy luxury of seeing myself in the bathroom mirror while bathing and, in the same perverse area, a succession of bathroom scales, the latest being a digital model which often flashes a readout saying, "You've got to be kidding!"

A succession of neckties that must have been unearthed by archeologists digging on the set of Broderick Crawford's old TV series, *Highway Patrol*.

A velvet double-breasted sport coat with leather buttons that Adolph Menjou wouldn't be caught dead in. (As a matter of sheer coincidence, I remember reading some years back in *Photoplay* that Adolph Menjou was found dead wearing nothing but a double-breasted velvet sport coat very much like the one my wife gave me. According to the Hollywood vice squad, the case is unsolved and still open.)

This year's offering was a silver (plastic) television set which she proudly exclaimed was "the size of a pair of binoculars." I presume she settled on this long-needed item after failing to find a pair of binoculars the size of a television set.

If there appears to be a trace of hostility or defensiveness in the above offered catalog of outrageous gifts, it may well be because several weeks have passed since our anniversary and I have yet to come up with my present to her.

Midway through this epic, it occurred to me that a specially dedicated twenty-fifth wedding anniversary column might be a unique and treasured gift, though its location in the op-ed pages would likely cause it to escape my apolitical bride's notice. (She once observed to someone who commented on the customary placement of this column, "I don't know why it's on those editorial pages. It's so misleading…people think he must have brains or something." In defense of her confusion, I should point out that when I once asked an editor whether he categorized my work as humor, satire, or social comment, I got the reply, "We like to think of it as 'extended filler.'")

And so, with the knowledge that desperation is the mother of aberrant behavior and the hope that this tribute will suffice as a twenty-fifth anniversary token, I dedicate it to the longstanding love of my life and banked but still smoldering fire of my loins, Lu Steed, and, in the words of that great American (I think it was Rick in *Casablanca* or the peeping Tom in *Porky's*), "Here's to looking at *you*, Kid!" (September 1983)

BLUNDER IN BERMUDA MATCHES BUSH'S GAFFE

According to the honking clamor in the British press recently, one would think that President Bush's recent contretemps with Queen Elizabeth caused a dip in U.S.-British relations approaching the strain that resulted when the Brits torched the White House some years back.

The presidential gaffe took place in London during the Group of Seven gathering when Mr. Bush had the temerity to—get this—sit down before Queen Elizabeth at a photo session preceding dinner at Buckingham Palace. The queen, appropriately aghast, glared at Mr. Bush until he got up, allowed her to take her seat, and then formally requested permission to sit down. Apparently, as a child, Mr. Bush never played "May I?"

I was completely sympathetic with the president in that just the week before I had committed a somewhat similar diplomatic blunder while speaking to a group in Bermuda. (I get invited to speak a lot. I don't get re-invited by the same group very often.) The speaking engagement was to a group of eight hundred American lawyers who were holding a meeting in Bermuda (after ruling out Cleveland by a voice vote), and I was informed that the premier, Sir John W. D. Swan, would be sitting at the head table and would make a few remarks prior to my talk.

Those in charge of the affair nervously gathered the head-table party in an anteroom before the banquet was to begin and told us in rigorous detail just how, accompanied by the music of the Bermuda military band, we were to proceed to the head table. It was very much like the lead-in at a high school prom without the spotlight and corsages.

As I was to sit on one side of the podium and Sir John on the other, we were designated as the leaders of our respective sides of the platform and were instructed to march in to the ballroom in two lines. I was to lead my line to the right side of and onto the head table and he was to take his to the left.

As we marched from the anteroom in the ballroom, I was suddenly confronted with three ballroom doors and, in a lady-or-the-tiger-like terror, bolted through the far right door only to run into a sea of people and tables crammed together cheek by jowl. As the music began I sensed it was too late to turn back and I began to lead my nervous little troop through the crush of tables, lifting our haunches over chair backs and making a herky-jerky serpentine path to the right side of the head table.

The premier, a veteran of these affairs, calmly waited with his group in the spacious main center aisle, having understood from the start that we were both to take that path before turning right and left.

Somehow, despite the fact that I had to force a path through the densely packed tables, and despite the fact that my wife (behind me in line) was hissing like a choleric goose that I was taking the wrong route, I made it to my side of the head table in what I'm sure was record time. My sturdy band of head-tablers was halfway up on the stage where I was being greeted by a good deal of enthusiastic applause from those who assumed I was the premier, when I realized he and his group were still at the starting gate waiting, as it turned out, for my group to show.

At that point, I did give way to a slight panic and ordered my confused crowd back off the platform until Sir John caught up. We finally came together at the head table and stood while the band blew through "The Star-Spangled Banner" and "God Save the Queen" (which, as best I can tell, is a direct rip-off of "My Country 'Tis of Thee" written, I think, by Hogey Carmichael in the 1940s.)

It's safe to say that my Marx Brothers maneuver was a breach of protocol and did cause some confusion or, as my wife so sympathetically put it to anyone who would listen following our return to Atlanta, "Rambo here just dorked right out. I mean, the premier must have been thinking, 'What a Goofus.'" I was, I confess, a little abashed by the episode and know just how Mr. Bush must have felt, but my victim, the premier, couldn't have been more gracious.

As for the querulous Queen Elizabeth, she should have just been glad that she was dealing with Mr. Bush and not Gerald R. Ford in the grip of one of his famous Chevy Chase imitations or, worse yet, the old Kissing Bandit Himself, Jimmy Carter, in full presidential pucker. (July 1991)

THE "CITY TOO BUSY TO HATE" SURE AIN'T TOO PROUD TO BRAG

The air in Atlanta and environs has been so incredibly hot and heavy of late that researchers at the world-renowned Cobb County Academy of Thermal Studies and Nude Dancing have mounted a massive inquiry to ascertain its cause.

Their study reveals that, in addition to Atlanta's traditional scorching July temperatures, the city's heat index (calculated by multiplying unsightly Braves fans without shirts times beers consumed per capita during a full nine-inning game) has been dangerously supercharged by hot air being generated by rampaging Olympic boosterism. Olympic officials claim that the Academy's revelations represent nothing more than sour grapes, citing Cobb County hostility generated by ACOG's rejection of proposals by the county that the games include drag racing, line dancing, and free-style cow-chip tossing.

It is a fact, however, that when it comes to self-aggrandizement and frequently recurring spasms of self-congratulation, the city of Atlanta takes a back seat to no one. It has always been, to use a country saying, "a hard dog to keep under the porch."

In a *Town and Country Magazine* in the 1960s, a staid citizen of the genteel (some say prissy) coastal city of Savannah characterized Atlanta as a "citadel of Babbitry." Indeed, Sinclair Lewis's relentless *Main Street* booster, George Babbitt, would find himself thrilled to the brink of incontinence with all the Olympic banners, billboards, and bluster.

Some observers, however, think that the impending Olympics have caused Atlanta's notorious capacity for blatant braggadocio to swell to previously unparalleled proportions. It is clear that the Olympic boosters are setting new levels of bombast. As Olympic Committee Chairman Billy Payne likes to say, the Games will be the biggest peacetime event in the 20th century with fifteen thousand athletes and coaches, two million spectators in Atlanta, and three billion spectators on TV (which, Olympic officials boast, is expected to exceed the number of moviegoers who shuck out $6.50 to see Demi Moore's bountiful balcony in *Striptease*).

ACOG brags that more countries will participate in the games than are currently in the United Nations, and another well-worn boast is that the Atlanta Olympics will constitute the largest gathering of nations in the history of the world, but this could change in late August when Demi Moore is scheduled to address the United Nations.

All of this causes some understandable cynicism from other areas of the state, and a rural Georgia citizen, having been exposed to all this magniloquence, was recently heard to say, "Atlanta, Atlanta. I'm sick and damn tired of hearing about Atlanta. If Atlanta could suck as hard as it can blow, the Atlantic Ocean would be in Newnan."

But to borrow another canine metaphor, "It's a sorry dog that won't wag its own tail." And if the Olympics go off according to Atlanta's ambitious plan, Billy Payne might well say of the city's Olympian endeavors, "If you can do it, it ain't bragging."

I know Demi would agree. (July 1996)

WHEN A WRISTWATCH COSTS $3,192, YOU CAN BET IT'S NO BUM'S TICKER

As I plowed through some sixteen pounds of Sunday paper, tacking carefully through the sea of cheery AIDS stories, the never-ending and numbing news from Nicaragua, and the flotsam and jetsam of gratuitous catalogs, which bob about in the waters that must be navigated in search of the wonderfully lurid and pulse-quickening lingerie ads, which would likely bring color to Hugh Hefner's sallow and sunken cheeks, I came upon what, at first blush, seemed to be a bargain of the first water for those seeking a status wristwatch. The advertisement bleated "Rolex" and "$133," causing my bargain-hunting juices to stir in greedy anticipation.

Though I myself have an aging but serviceable $125 Accutron ("Railroad Approved") timepiece, I was tempted by the offer, as I am not unaware that there exists considerable status in owning certain watches, and that high in the pantheon of these showpieces is the mighty Rolex.

In the wake (hold on, queasy reader, and we'll soon sail through these tiresome nautical metaphors, which—the nurse thinks—were brought on by a mild overdose of Cutty Sark) of the spiritual soap opera offered by Jim and Tammy Faye Bakker and their pastoral peccadillos, the legendary panache of the Rolex was even acknowledged in song as Ray Stevens posed the musical question, "Would Jesus Wear a Rolex on His Television Show?"

The rhetorical barb, as all of us who follow the plethora of televangelists now infesting the airwaves know, was directed at the Right Reverend James (Jimmy) Swaggart, whose shiny Rolex approximates the size of a weather station in Greenland and is thought by some to be a bit gaudy for a man of the cloth. (Though Jimmy, in his own defense, points out tersely that some cloth can be right gaudy too, indicating tattersall and madras, to, in his words, "name just a few.")

I don't want to get drawn into any ideological arguments on the question of appropriate timepieces for our spiritual leaders (though I would observe in passing that it would be difficult for the pope to tote a pocket watch). I just brought up the subject in the first place (for those of you who haven't abandoned this exposition altogether in search of the lingerie ads) to say that I was mildly tempted to spring for $133 worth of status. A closer reading of the ad copy, however, revealed to my incredulous eye (the right one is incredulous, the left believes almost everything it sees, including, for example, World Federation Wrestling and claims by cable TV hucksters that "fortunes can be made by buying foreclosed real estate with no money down"), that this overstuffed stainless-steel and gold status symbol was going down not for $133 but for $133 per month, for 24 months, which, unless my multiplication is off, comes to a tidy $3,192 (plus applicable sales tax).

Now, I'm as much for status as the next man (maybe even more, as I note that the next man is wearing one of those digital watches found at truck-stop counters that pulses "Go Dawgs" every second), but three grand for a watch that is fat, heavy, and ugly, to boot, is going a bit too far for me.

Consequently, I'm advising those status seekers who come clamoring to my chambers for counsel to buy a Timex and use their savings to

(a) invest in a pair of Gucci loafers and wear them without socks (nothing says status like hairy ankles and little gold dingles on your shoes),

(b) rent a car phone, which you can do for less than $133 a month, and impress the stew out of other motorists who think you're doing big deals when you're really just trying to be caller No. 10 on some radio station and win free tickets to a water slide in Smyrna; or

(c) have your VW Beetle fitted out with one of those Rolls Royce fronts and get a little yellow sign for the window that says "Dork on Board" (maybe with a Rolls Royce front you won't even need the sign).

Besides, you really don't deserve too much status if you have to buy your watch "on time." (There may be a pun in there somewhere, but we'll just have to wait for it to surface.) (June 1987)

I WAS ABOUT TO GO BATTY, BUT A NEW CAUSE SAVED ME

I found myself wallowing in a slough of despair the other evening (an activity that is not only depressing but which, done to excess, can wrinkle the devil out of your suit). When questioned by my querulous spouse as to why I was "moping around," I confided that I was terribly concerned about the lack of new causes these days.

I told her that I sensed our country's activists were becoming increasingly jaded with saving the whales, keeping the baby seals from having their ears boxed, fighting presidential parkways, boycotting lettuce, grapes and the like, and I asked dolefully, "Where are the new areas of cosmic concern coming from?"

"Maybe they should start a campaign to keep people from ending their concerns with prepositions," she sniffed callously as she dived back into her TV dinner.

The following morning as I sat in my chambers in the grip of a continuing funk, in burst my law partner and friend, Byron "Whiplash" Attridge, waving a sheaf of correspondence that caused my dolorous anxiety to give way to a burst of hope and happiness. Attridge, while opening his morning mail, had come across a form letter with enclosures that he knew I would find of interest. It was a communiqué from Dr. Merlin D. Tuttle, founder and science director of Bat Conservation International, Inc. (BCI), thanking Attridge for his "interest in bats" and enclosing valuable information about the threats facing bats here and abroad.

Attridge, disclaiming any activist leanings, was puzzled as to how his name got on the mailing list until I reminded him that in the 1950s at Princeton he had led a vigorous protest against the wearing of seersucker suits before Easter and even now was a regular contributor of heated, if somewhat incomprehensible, letters to the editor deploring the graduated income tax.

Relieved that the nation's best minds were still coming up with fresh causes for our country's ever eager activists, I plunged happily into Tuttle's package, and my attention was immediately riveted by a slick brochure featuring a photo of two upside down bats under Tuttle's plaintive and rhetorical query, "Why save bats?"

Well, just to ask the question is to answer it. Tuttle points out that bats are among the most important seed-dispensing animals in the tropical rain forests and have greatly influenced the survival of many fruits, nuts, spices, and derivatives from plants such as guavas, carob, peaches, and tequila. Frankly, I think some nuts shouldn't survive or, if they do, they ought to lay off the tequila.

Tuttle goes on to extol the virtues of bat guano as a major source of fertilizer and then testily debunks a number of common myths about bats by asserting that:

1. They are not rodents.
2. They are not blind and do not "become entangled in people's hair."
3. They seldom have rabies.

The good doctor carefully avoids mention of some of my primary concerns in the area:

1. That guys with slicked back hair, capes, and black eye liner often turn themselves into bats and suck the juice out of your neck while you're sleeping.
2. They are bad to clog up one's belfry.

Lest the unwary should think that bat conservation is only an American dilemma, the BCI letterhead boasts a Scientific Advisory Board with representatives from, among others, Czechoslovakia, India, the United Kingdom, and, as further evidences of glasnost, the redoubtable Dr. Irina K. Rakhmatulina of the United Soviet Socialist Republics. If there is a chapter in Transylvania, no mention is made of it on the letterhead.

Accompanying the letter and brochure is the Bat Conservation International 1987/1988 Catalog featuring an etching of the Spotted Bat ($50 for non-members; $45 for members), bat jewelry, and, of course, bat T-shirts and videocassettes. I kept looking for a catchy bumper sticker saying something like "Lugosi Lives!"

When I excitedly suggested to Attridge that he could leap on the bat bandwagon and, as suggested in the enclosed pledge card, become a supporting member in the $1,000 category, he left very abruptly. Like, as Dr. Tuttle in his jocular way might say, a bat out of hell. (June 1988)

Bob and Miz Mac at a book signing

FROM ALL THE GANG AT HALLMARK

For those of you who don't keep up with the obscure but, I'm sure, profitable celebratory events dreamed up by brainstorming executives of the greeting card industry, this is National Secretaries Week. ("Listen to this, Chief. What about 'National Crossing Guards Day' or maybe a week honoring your neighborhood proctologist, like, 'When the hospital gown starts to fall, I keep my back against the wall'?")

How, you may ask, do I know that this week is National Secretaries Week? The answer is simple. My trusted and efficient secretary of long standing, Yvonne "That file's been lost for years" McMillian, never fails to give me advance and pointed notice followed by fulsome particulars on how other bosses are planning to honor their secretaries with lunches, gifts, cash bonuses, days off, etc.

This year was no exception as Yvonne "Does this letter really have to go out today?" McMillian issued the annual alert she has been giving me since she signed on as a sassy, red-haired eighteen-year-old in 1963.

As she stood there expectantly, obviously willing to interrupt her morning marathon of nail buffing and personal phone calls to make reservations at an expensive restaurant, I began to wax nostalgic about her thirty-plus years of secretarial service.

She came to our chambers fresh from the prestigious Marsh Business School (whose seal bore the Latin phrase *Carpe maxim* ["Let them get their own damn coffee"]), where she excelled at long lunch hours and talking back.

I vividly remember calling one of her references, a secretarial sciences teacher at South Cobb High, who seemed excessive in her praise of Yvonne's personality. It turned out, to our dismay after Yvonne was hired, that "good personality" was a code phrase for "She can't type a lick."

She was assigned to me and Lawyer Hurst, who was my senior, and we loaded her down with a mountain of accumulated work. The spunky young employee worked for eight hours straight and then turned in her resignation. Lawyer Hurst, in a spasm of avuncular advice, told her that she would regret such a decision for the rest of her life and convinced her to stay. She never forgave him.

However, she learned to type up a storm and mastered all the other secretarial skills, such as taking the blame for her boss's errors, lying on the phone as to his availability or whereabouts, doing his children's tax returns, performing all manner of personal errands his wife assumed he was doing, etc. My eyes brimmed as I suddenly became aware of all she had done for me over those three decades and, in a spontaneous but uncharacteristic outburst, I blurted, "Miz Mac, what would you do if I told you that you were responsible for what I am today?" Fixing me with a baleful stare, she replied, "I guess I'd just have to learn to live with it."

Yvonne, from me and all the gang at Hallmark ("For those who care enough to buy a card rather than thinking up their own greetings"), Happy National Secretaries Week. (April 1994)

Bob with son Josh (left) and son-in-law Burton Vance at Augusta National Golf Club

FOR GOLFERS, JUST TRYING TO DECODE "THE SECRET" IS PAR FOR THE COURSE

Oscar Wilde once described the sport of foxhunting as "the unspeakable in hot pursuit of the inedible." Modernizing and paraphrasing, one might describe golf as "the uncoordinated in dogged pursuit of the unachievable."

There are, to be sure, a small knot of golf's practitioners who do achieve a slippery and temporal grip on the slithery sport and sometimes shoot par. Those people are referred to by wannabe golfer Lewis Grizzard as "knowing The Secret." Mr. Grizzard, upon seeing a par golfer in action, will mutter knowingly and bitterly, "He's one of 'em. He knows The Secret," certain but unhappy in the knowledge that the par golfer would rather have his appendix removed with rusty niblick than share "The Secret" with the rest of us.

Only a race of people as dour and ascetic as the Scots could have conceived an enterprise as masochistic as golf. The term itself derives from the Caledonian word "golffe," meaning incredible pain, public humiliation, or making a serious speech to a Daughters of the American Revolution convention with your fly open.

Why reasonably intelligent adults submit themselves so relentingly to its rigors ranks with other mysteries of cosmic consequence such as:

1. Is TV wrestling fake?
2. What is the average IQ of those people who put little stuffed animals with suction cups for paws on their car windows?

Not only is the sport itself a multinational obsession, recent forecasts by the internationally renowned Cobb County School of Economics, Electrolysis, and Bikini Waxing predict that by the year 2000 more than half of our gross national product will be spent on golf equipment and related accoutrements such as head covers for putters, Day-Glo colored knickers, golf balls of incredibly bilious hues, golf bags sufficient in size to house a family of boat people, and high-tech golf clubs with shafts made from everything from berylium (a new miracle alloy made of barium enemas, aluminum, and ground-up Toyota parts) to radioactive waste.

The incredible eagerness of rabid golfers to spend money on the craze knows no bounds. Early reports indicate that a newly released book on golf—*Does a Wild Bear Chip in the Woods?*—by the previously mentioned Muse of Moreland, Lewis Grizzard, himself a twelve-handicapper, are selling like hotcakes (this in spite of the fact that one reviewer claimed the syrup and butter made it a "messy read").

If I may be permitted a personal aside, I would mention that Mr. Grizzard (ever alert for extended filler) included in the book an unexpurgated reprint of an article on golf from *Augusta Magazine* written by my brother, Michael Parker Steed (actually the article was printed in block letters with crayon, but I'm coming to that).

"Mike," as we call him, deserves all the encouragement we can give him. Just two years ago, we learned he was addicted to those letters in *Penthouse* magazine and we had to send him to Tifton to the Georgia Baptist Home for the Easily Aroused. At one point he had read so many of those letters he couldn't even lick a stamp without getting keyed up. He's back on the streets now, a bit tense but otherwise fully recovered, and the magazine article reprinted in Mr. Grizzard's book was thought to be a major breakthrough in his treatment.

Where will this golf-a-mania end? Probably not even savants as wise as Hugh Downs can say, but in the meantime, we should all heed the cosmic counsel of that great philosopher Descartes (I think it was Descartes. It was either Descartes or Chi Chi Rodriguez.) who said, "Keep your head down and replace all divots." (June 1990)

A RIBITING LOOK AT A TOADALLY ABSURD PHENOMENON IN ENGLAND

Since the Atlanta papers first began covering Dixie like the dew several years after the Beginning of Time, irate politicians, owners of purported major league franchises, and chicken lovers everywhere have been heard to utter the recurring war cry, "Them lying Atlanta newspapers!" To those muttering malcontents I say, "Lying Atlanta newspapers? What about the lying *Wall Street Journal*?"

Actually, I never said that to any of those choleric and foam-flecked souls. Ever eager to avoid any sort of confrontation that might lead to physical pain, my approach is usually to smile and reply, "Well, I wouldn't know. I only read *Grit* and the *Christian Science Monitor*."

However, while I didn't say it, I did think it about *The Wall Street Journal* when I read a recent article in its stolid pages on the perilous sex habits of British toads. The front-page story by

"Glynn Mapes" (obviously a fake name) bore the dateline of "Henley-on-Thomas, England" and contained the war-raising revelation that every March, "some twenty million tons of toads are run over by cars" while crossing public roadways to nearby breeding ponds.

Actually, in partial defense of *The Journal*, the twenty million tons of toads figure came from unnamed "toad experts." (Imagine the unmitigated shame endured by a parent who, when asked by well-meaning friends what their son is doing for a living, must look them in the eye and say, "Actually, Nigel is a toad expert." Is it any wonder the British are thought to be in such a precipitous general decline?)

According to *The Journal*, the annual toad squashing is a dreadful carnage that makes a sickening and dangerous mess of the highways. However, one man's carnage is another man's cause, and the account goes on to report that in the United Kingdom alone, some four thousand volunteers of the International Toads on the Roads Society muck about the roadways in rubber boots using plastic pails to carry the endangered toads to safety.

My guess is that these people are on the waiting lists as potential protesters for the baby seal, the Presidential Parkway, and anti-veal-cutlet protest movements that are currently so overburdened with eager volunteers that they have had to temporarily close their membership ranks.

Enterprising Toad on the Roaders have also constructed six toad tunnels under selected highways to reduce the slithery slaughter.

But back to the question of honesty in journalism and the reporting of the slippery statistic that twenty million tons of toads are run over by cars during the mating season every March. My bean-counting banker friend, Linden "Double Entry" Longino, took *The Journal* to task by pointing out in an unacknowledged and unpublished letter to their editors that twenty million tons of toads is, to quote his own mild understatement, "a lot of toads."

It is, by his calculation, forty billion pounds, to be precise, and, estimating twenty toads to the pound, he reckons that eight hundred billion toads are crushed annually in England during the mating season. And, as he cogently points out, these are just the ones that fatefully find themselves "between the treads on the ribiting road to love."

Longino continues with the pencil-pushing persistence of a skeptical and gimlet-eyed banker: Assuming that only twenty percent of the horny toads are crushed in their passage over the roads (eight hundred billion toads), the annual population would equal four trillion toads. With this frightful horror afoot, my guess is that Margaret Thatcher didn't resign, she fled the country while there was still time.

The relentless Longino, by now drenched in sweat but still hunched over his Hewlett-Packard, summed up his incredulity with this felicitous observation: "It is intuitively obvious to even the most casual observer of nature that the experts you quoted must be bull frogs. If four trillion two-inch long toads formed an off-road chorus line, this happy host of hopeful horny hoppers would wrap around the world five thousand times—croaking for self sex."

Like I said, that lying *Wall Street Journal*—sex, lies, and toad-ally absurd! (June 1991)

WILL AN "OPERATION DESERT STORM" BE NEEDED TO HALT SWISS CONQUEST OF THE WORLD?

I don't want readers to think that I'm off on some sort of vendetta ("vendetta"—n. 1. Vengeful quarrel; 2. Italian economy car introduced unsuccessfully after World War II) against *The Wall Street Journal*. After all, it's easy to pick on a newspaper with no sports page, comics, or Ann Landers and whose idea of a dynamite, above-the-fold headline is "Hennessy Is Retiring at Allied Signal Sooner than Expected."

Even though my recent column debunking claims by the *WSJ* to the effect that eighty billion toads are squashed annually as they cross British roadways to nearby breeding ponds is being quietly promoted for a Pulitzer, I have no ambitions to undertake some sort of jihad against the trusty old business chronicle.

However, I would be derelict if I didn't point out that an increasing number of bubbles of unreality and sensationalism have begun to come to the surface on the pages of that once staid and reliable newspaper.

Following its toadally absurd coverage of the lethal British frog migration, *The Wall Street Journal* reported with, as far as we can tell, a straight face that the Swiss government had contracted with McDonnell Douglas Corp. to purchase thirty-four F/A-18 Hornet jet fighters for its military arsenal.

"What," astounded readers must be asking, "military arsenal?" I think it's common knowledge that except for the Swiss Army knife and a few guys dressed in funny costumes guarding the Vatican, Switzerland has no "military arsenal."

In fact, serious students of history will remember that in 1712, the crowned heads of Europe gathered in Zurich to enter into a pact that granted the Swiss a global monopoly on milk chocolate and yodeling in exchange for renouncing all territorial claims and disbanding its military machine (the so-called "Honda Accord").

My guess, and I hate to say this, is that *The Wall Street Journal*, fearful of competition from other newspapers whose front pages are literally awash in color charts, pie graphs, and opinion polls, is simply making a lot of this stuff up.

If their dangerous trend continues, we may soon see *The Journal* at grocery-store checkout lines featuring banner headlines screaming: "Iaccoca Out of Closet! Admits Owning a Toyota." Or, "Space Aliens from Distant Galaxy Corner Pork Bellies Market." Or, "Alan Greenspan Confesses: 'I Was Elvis's Love Slave.'"

I don't want to draw any conclusions until my research staff/secretary, Yvonne "That File's Been Lost for Years" McMillian, has had a chance to check out the Switzerland entry in her children's World Book Encyclopedia, but it does appear that the *WSJ* is playing fast and loose with the news in an attempt to hype its sales.

On the other hand, what a dark and grisly business it would be to find out that the reports on Switzerland were true and that while the rest of the nations of the world are busy beating their swords into plowshares, VCRs, and cheap cars, those wonderful folks who gave us *The Sound of Music* are secretly arming themselves to the teeth with dreams of territorial expansion.

For all we know, Gen. H. Norman Schwarzkopf may, even now, be girding his considerable loins to repulse a Swiss incursion into neighboring countries..."Operation Dessert Storm." Today Liechtenstein, tomorrow the world. (July 1991)

CHATTY CHASTAIN AUDIENCES NEED SOME GAG RULES

We currently find ourselves in the grip of urban unrest, civil disorder, and borderline anarchy. I'm not referring to the crisis in the inner cities; I'm speaking of the yahoos at Chastain Park who persist in talking and talking and talking throughout the course of the evening concerts there.

Those who say that the art of conversation is dying obviously haven't attended a summer concert at Chastain Park recently.

A few evenings back, we were the eager guests of our friend Lawyer Ragsdale who had managed a prime table at Chastain for the Harry Connick Jr. concert. My sinewy spouse of longstanding was so enthusiastic at the prospect of seeing and hearing the stud muffin Connick perform that she had volunteered to furnish the entree for the event. Our taste buds were dazzled by her gourmet meatloaf sandwich recipe (take two pieces of white bread, slather with mayonnaise, add meatloaf—serves one).

Mr. Connick took the stage at the designated hour and launched with enthusiasm into his mellow and lively big band, high-energy performance. But our rapture was incomplete as the six-some at the table in front of us persisted in their high-decibel conversations on the apparent assumption that Mr. Connick had been imported to furnish background music for their gabbing and gorging.

One of their number, who was particularly garrulous, punctuated his non-stop talking with occasional explosions of laughter that sounded like a camel coughing up a fur ball. All this despite the fact that the master of ceremonies had asked everyone to hold down on the talking, and Mr. Connick himself, at the beginning of his performance (manfully holding his head erect despite what appeared to be a firkin of styling gel), had pleaded with the crowd to not talk, or, as he said, "If you must talk, then shout at each other so I'll think you're shouting for me."

The chin-music ensemble at the next table was unfazed by all this importuning, chiefly because they were talking relentlessly and heard none of it. The other concert goers at the tables in our area were, to their credit, as quiet as mice. (They don't call me the "Sultan of Simile" for nothing.)

Midway through the concert, my frustration overcame my reluctance to act like a prissy hall monitor, and I leaned over to the braying bunch at the next table and, pointing to Lawyer Ragsdale, said to one of their number, "Pardon me, but this fellow is on a twenty-four-hour furlough from the Georgia State Institute for the Violent and Criminally Insane. This is his only chance to hear a concert this summer and your loud talking is beginning to agitate him some."

Happily, my admonition did not fall on entirely deaf ears, and for the remainder of the concert our noisy neighbors made some attempt at holding their conversation down to the level of infield chatter at a baseball game. One pretty blonde in their group even turned her chair around and watched the concert for a while.

Emboldened by my small success, I am now assaying the possibility of writing an insert for the Chastain Park programs that would offer a number of rejoinders, remonstrations, and requests that could be used by other Chastain concertgoers (ninety percent of whom, by the way, do not talk during a performance) to subdue their rude and loquacious neighbors.

A few early entries are:

- "If the music is interfering with your conversation, perhaps we could ask the band to leave."
- "Is there a volume control on your group?"
- "Did you know that talking during a concert is a sign of sexual insecurity?"
- "Pardon me, I believe your manners are leaking."
- "If you don't quiet down, the concert vigilantes are going to kick your behind so bad you'll be walking around on your elbows."
- "If you don't can that palaver, you're going to be wearing that candelabra like a pair of antlers."
- "Hey! Shut up!"

It's just one concertgoer's small attempt at addressing a much larger problem, but as the philosopher Arthur Schopenhauer once said (in a aphorism marvelously apt for Chastain Park concerts), "If everyone lit just one little candle, we'd be up to our butts in hot wax." (June 1992)

LEARNING THE INS AND OUTS OF THE HIGH-FASHION WORLD

Well, I don't know about you, but I'm convinced that fashion rules the world. I know it has been a major influence in my life.

From the time I was but a pup I always harbored a burning ambition (which, on occasion, throbbed as well) to pursue a career in the field of spot cleaning and blocking hats. I had even managed to obtain a full scholarship to the then-famous L'Ecole de Chapeau in Cuthbert, Alabama, when lightning struck the world of fashion with the pronouncement that the bare-headed John F. Kennedy had rendered hats as dead as soccer.

Taken by surprise and bitterly disappointed, I grimly vowed that I would never again be left cold and goose-fleshed sitting in the fashion tub after the water had drained. True to that resolve, from that day to this I have remained, in the words of even my severest foes, "incredibly *au courant*" by devouring every issue of that bible of style and fashion to which my sinewy spouse so avidly subscribes, *W*.

This incredibly trendy arbiter of taste and good grooming is published bimonthly under an assumed name by its unlikely parent, *Women's Wear Daily*, a frumpy trade journal for those in the rag business. Over the years *W* has kept me on the cutting edge of the world of fashion, which is known to be subject to whimsy and caprice (not to be confused with the Cobb County interior decorating firm by the same name).

Presented in living color in a full-sized newspaper format, *W* is perfect reading material for fashion-minded socialites who need to be on the crest of every fashion wave but find *Vogue*, *Harper's Bazaar*, and the like—"with all that writing"—just too taxing mentally.

Eschewing text for the most part, *W* deals almost exclusively in photographs depicting what might be described by unsophisticated readers as "lifestyles of the rich and fatuous," captured as they caper about in their native habitat—society balls, restaurant or disco openings, coming outs of horsey looking debutantes, and a glittering and never ending succession of similar self-congratulatory events.

Inside pages reveal the same old faces in new ensembles, like Nancy Kissinger plowing through the high-society seas with the foot shorter and ever-dour Henry following in her wake looking like a dyspeptic troll who has been flushed from under a bridge wearing a tuxedo, and the ubiquitous Pat (Mrs. William F.) Buckley who is featured so relentlessly that one suspects if she fails to appear in a single issue, the publication will lose its bulk-mailing permit.

My favorite *W* feature is the annual issue in which its editors reveal to a breathlessly expectant constituency of social lions from Sutton Place to East Marietta, just what is "In" and "Out" for the year. Until I am able to clasp this definitive work to my anxious bosom, I, like all other *W* readers, am simply suspended in an opinionless fashion limbo.

In this year's fashion and style *pronunciamiento*, *W* decreed that bosoms are "in," though, from the accompanying photos, it seems clear that to be "in" they must be worn "out." Also "in" are Elizabeth Taylor (and her grand Tetons), "being naughty at lunch" (which I take to mean staging food fights, drinking iced tea with the spoon still protruding from the glass, and burping over one's demitasse), virginity (unless you're really being naughty at lunch), dancing the cha-cha, and—get this—"wearing fake honorary decorations that turn over to reveal a photo of your dog."

W deemed the following to be "out": breast implants, which, from the look of the high-fashion women in its pages, have been replaced by shoulder implants, aerobics, Sean Penn, Australia, the Rev. Pat Robertson, "overgrown cities, like Atlanta," wine coolers, and, to prove that *W* is not just fashion froth for simple-minded trend spotters but really has a social conscience, "increasing executive salaries when a company is laying off employees." Workers of the world, unite! You have nothing to lose but your Guccis.

Finally, the editors have established a fashion-and-style purgatory so extreme that it is designated as "The Out Palace" into whose nether regions they have summarily banished "Vanna White, Mario Cuomo, smoking between courses [which, apparently, is *de classe* even when trying to be "naughty at lunch"], and Prince Philip and hoop earrings." Frankly, I never really liked Prince Philip in those hoop earrings either.

So, style-setters, the next time you're having one of those scruffy days when you feel like the world's a tuxedo and you're a pair of brown Hush Puppies, just snuggle up to a copy of *W*. You'll be glad you did. (March 1987)

GETTING A MUSICAL EARFUL: BECAUSE LIKE, MAN, THAT'S WHAT ROCK 'N' ROLL IS ALL ABOUT

Ever the unwitting and bumbling victim of cruel circumstances, I recently found myself at the Omni in a boiling mass of barely post-pubescents attending a raucous concert performed by the oddly named Bon Jovi. An unhappy combination of gullibility and inattentiveness always causes me to be the constant dupe of my wiry wife's mercurial musical tastes.

In fact, through lack of attention on my part to her capricious planning and invitation accepting, I had gone from Scylla to Charybdis in the Omni in a span of just four days, having been a casualty of a Hank Williams Jr. concert on a Saturday and the Bon Jovi musical mayhem the following Wednesday. Correctly judging that reflections on "Why me, Lord?" would not help me get through the musical ordeal that lay ahead, I busied myself comparing the crowds in which we had found ourselves engulfed.

The contrast was startling. The crowd at the Hank Williams Jr. concert looked like a casting call for the love scene from *Deliverance*. They were a flint-eyed, beefy, and grizzled herd bedecked in camouflage outfits and Confederate memorabilia. The Bon Jovi aficionados, on the other hand, were an appealing, very young, well-scrubbed lot heavy into miniskirts that looked to have been applied with paintbrushes or jeans that were so amply stuffed they looked as though they had been jumped into from a high place.

Their general appearance was remarkably attractive, save only the occasional young male whose ear lamentably sported an earring. I longed to point out to each of them that Willie Nelson never had a hit record after he had his ears pierced but sensed that my message would fall on deaf lobes.

Except for two suspicious-looking taxpayers in their forties with fedoras, shades, and dark suits who were apparently doing a bad "Blues Brothers" impression, I was the only gray-haired, neck-tied music lover in the place. In fact, as I came through the turnstile, a middle-aged ticket taker cracked at me, "You heard Guy Lombardo was dead, didn't you, Bud? It was in all the papers."

As is always the case, we were treated to a warm-up act, which, in this case, consisted of four anorexic and gratuitously bellicose teenagers aptly named Skid Row. Their routine, which looked like the Bataan Death March set to music, featured an endless amount of incomprehensible caterwauling.

They all wore tattered blue jeans and shoulder length hair and looked like the children that Don Knotts refuses to discuss. Their upper arms were so spiderlike that the tattoos affected by some of them could only have been accomplished with microscopes.

Between their mind-numbing musical selections, they offered in language so foul that it would make Richard Pryor blanch a philosophy for teenagers roughly as follows: "If like your boss, or your parents, like, or your teacher, like gets on your case and tells you what to do, well then, like, just tell them to go [expletive phrase suggesting an anatomically impossible act deleted] themselves. Because, like, man, that's what rock 'n' roll is all about."

"Well," I huffed to my zoned-out spouse, "I don't remember Pat Boone saying that's what rock 'n' roll was all about." Unfortunately, she cannot read lips and my protest was completely lost in the ongoing cacophony.

At length, Skid Row's barrage of trashy talk and death-defying decibels abated, and we were treated to the obligatory forty-five-minute wait while the stage was reset for the featured attraction. I can never understand why so much time and attention is given to this intermezzo in that all that is required in the way of instrumentation are extension cords and wall sockets.

During this interval the Bon Jovi roadies did what is benignly called a "sound check" with recorded music. As best I can tell, this consists of nothing more than turning up the volume on the tractor-trailer size speakers to insure that the streetlights dim as far as Marietta and that everyone in the first twenty rows of the Omni is bleeding steadily from the nose and ears.

Amid fireworks and blinding light, Bon Jovi suddenly materialized on stage. Except for their keyboard pummeler, who looked like the illicit love child of Phyllis Diller and the Phantom of the Opera, they were a far better-looking bunch than Skid Row.

Curiously, all of their T-shirts, posters, and record albums featured the words "New Jersey" in letters of equal size and prominence following "Bon Jovi." I have known many people from New Jersey but none who would admit it so readily. It is a well-documented fact that when the Playboy clubs opened in New Jersey, the bunnies dressed in rat suits.

Though I had not heard any of their selections previously, I must confess that on balance their concert was a very entertaining and lively display. And, at times, their back beat got so basic that my toe began to tap involuntarily, causing the children in my vicinity to roll their eyes at me and gape as though Dame Margaret Rutherford had suddenly broken into a buck and wing.

As my grizzled spouse and I pulled the cotton from our ears and joined the sated crowd flowing toward the exits, it occurred to me that I still didn't know if Bon Jovi was the name of the lead singer or the name of the group. When I ventured to ask, my wife, who is so old that when she went to college foreign language was still a required course, said tersely, "*Bon Jovi* is French for *good Jovi*."

That was when I put the cotton back in my ears. (March 1989)

PURPLE PRINCE CAN'T MATCH MUSIC MONARCHS OF THE PAST

If all those letters to *Penthouse* magazine were set to music, what you would have is a Prince concert. If you crossed Robin Hood in purple tights with a lookout for a massage parlor, what you'd have is Prince himself.

For reasons that I can't recall and perhaps never fully understood, I went to the Omni with my aging rock 'n' roll wife to see and painfully hear the vaunted Lovesexy World (No Cameras) Tour '88 featuring Prince (no last name).

I must admit that on one level I was a willing participant. After hearing so much about him, I was more than a little curious as to why a rock singer who was apparently named after a dog and who looked like an anorexic Little Richard was the subject of so much attention and adulation. I came away with ringing ears, but otherwise unenlightened.

After a carnal and noisy two-and-one-half hours, I determined that Mr. Prince, a native of Minneapolis (one of the first places you'd think to go if you were looking for a sex symbol), is one of those folks who gives vulgarity a bad name.

Performing in the round before a packed and enthusiastic house, the Prince pranced in five-inch heels (as far as I could tell he was not wearing pantyhose) and walked a line between lubricity and spirituality or, as he himself put it so eloquently, "It's easy to be nasty; what's hard is being perfect in the eyes of God." This breathtakingly trenchant truth was piously uttered after an hour of song and dance so nasty as to bring a blush to the sallow cheeks of Dr. Ruth.

But, again using the *Penthouse* metaphor, each issue apparently needs a socially redeeming insert to stay just shy of crossing the pornographic point of no return, thus avoiding possible criminal prosecution. Where is Hinson McAuliffe when we really need him?

Prince's shift from the salaciously secular to the spiritual realm consisted of a few gratuitous gospel numbers such as, "It Is No Secret What God Can Do" and "I Wish You Heaven," bringing to my mind the eternal verity in the old black spiritual, "Everybody Talking 'Bout Heaven Ain't Going There."

All of this pseudo-sanctimonious stuff was interspersed with coital pantomime that would make the casual observer think that some Broadway impresario has assayed to set a sex manual to music. These maneuvers, for the most part, were performed by Prince and three lascivious ladies wearing what appeared to be orthopedic black garter belts from Frederick's of Smyrna. One of the trio was so beefy she looked like Tina Turner on steroids.

The entire concupiscent concert was accompanied by so much special lighting and so many speakers that the lights in the metro area must have dimmed when the concert cranked up.

If the Prince is interested in my opinion (and you'd be surprised at how many rock stars slip into my chambers from time to time seeking counsel), I would tell him what his program needs is some punctuation. There is absolutely no way the unschooled ear can determine when one song ends and the other begins. I thought the first half of the show was just one long tune with a variety of prurient prancing. Actually, I learned later that there were probably eight or nine different tunes involved, but only the cognoscenti can tell where one stops and the other starts.

All of this business is performed in more billowing smoke and purple gas than a large pulp mill could generate. I hope the promoters were required to file an environmental impact study before staging the concert.

It was a memorable show and worth attending just for the crowd reaction, but I don't think today's raunchy royalty is any match for the musical monarchs of the past—say Count Basie or Duke Ellington. (October 1988)

WHERE DO THEY DREDGE UP THOSE FOLKS WHO APPEAR IN INFOMERCIAL AUDIENCES?

No sooner than Speaker Newt Gingrich came down from Mount Kennesaw bearing stone tablets graven with the "Contract With America" did there arise a cry from every nook and cranny (not to be confused with a small Marietta law firm by the same name) clamoring for changes to the contract.

Like the old gospel song "Everybody Wants to Go to Heaven but Nobody Wants to Die," the righteous aware are eager for reform so long as it doesn't empty any trough from which they have been furiously feeding. I think Congress should immediately launch hearings on those studio audiences who show up for television infomercials and determine what laws can be passed to keep members of those audiences from getting married and reproducing or, worse yet, getting licenses to operate heavy machinery and equipment on public thoroughfares.

A number of serious questions need to be addressed in this regard, such as:

- Where do they dredge up those folks who appear in infomercial audiences? Are they paid? Are they given any mind-altering drugs which might explain their hand-clapping, foot-stomping enthusiasm for miracle cleaners, cookware, space-age mops, etc.?
- Is there any connection between someone who would serve as a studio audience member for an infomercial and those pitiful tourists who wander around in stretch pants and running shoes, carrying their valuables in what looks like a canvas colostomy bag strapped to their waists?

The producers of the infomercials are obviously doing something to whip the audiences into a state which ultimately causes foam to fleck their withers. I speculate that if the collective applause reaches a certain volume level, handlers come out of the wings and throw bits of fish or beef jerky to the audience. The crowds who sign up for the infomercials I have seen look like they would turn up for a root canal if it involved free tickets and snacks of some sort.

I can hear the dialogue now: "No, you have to write in earlier for tickets to the Letterman show. However, we do have some good seats left for an infomercial in which a glabrous goober from the audience volunteers to come on stage and have his bald spot spray painted with an aerosol can."

An extraordinarily high percentage of infomercials seem to involve the peddling of skin or hair products. Aging starlet Victoria Principal seems to be on every other channel flogging some eponymous unguents so extraordinary they require thirty minutes of sustained talking to explain. The poor woman has a concern with moist skin which borders on the obsessive.

In the hair category, the most recent infomercials flooding the airwaves are those that have to do with hanging little pieces of fake hair in a woman's regular hair to fluff up her do. They had these same things when I was in high school, but they never caught on because of an unfortunate marketing decision to call them "rats." Now, nothing seems to light up an infomercial studio audience more than some self-satisfied huckster pulling eight or ten rats out of an old lady's hair.

As my wife (the leathery language butcher) said when summing up a particularly bad movie (it was Robert Altman's *Ready to Wear* for those of you who still have a chance to avoid it), "I've got just two words for all that—*in sane*." (March 1995)

BUSINESS TYPES NEED TO GIVE UP ON THE THOUGHT OF DRESSING DOWN

Though newspapers are generally loath to report good news, I am pleased to be able to reveal that the homeless problem in downtown Atlanta is not as acute as previously reported.

A recent study by the prestigious Cobb County Institute of Social Studies and Transmission Exchange revealed that almost sixty percent of the group thought to be shabbily dressed, down-and-out vagrants are actually lawyers, accountants, and businessmen taking part in the odious and growing phenomenon known as "Casual Day." For reasons no one can fathom, this pernicious custom has been instigated in a number of offices and is becoming a swelling tide like raw Atlanta sewage in the Chattahoochee. Once a week, formerly well-groomed citizens have begun looking like hobos during the severest days of the Great Depression.

Inquiring minds ask, "What's the point? Why should someone attempting to charge clients hundreds of dollars an hour show up looking like he's been sleeping in a dumpster?"

I can't speak for the reasoning of the CPAs and business people, but as for the lawyers, there is abundant clinical material in my office building in the form of three law firms that have instituted the policy in what I believe to be an effort to counteract the stereotypical "stuffy" image of lawyers.

While all of them don't look like the homeless, they do in their various forms of mufti look pitiful. Once the line formerly held by those in suits and ties has been breached, there appears to be no going back. The casual dressers find themselves like Mohammed's coffin, suspended between attempts at being well-groomed or donning garb so outrageous it would test the gag reflexes of Hart, Schaffner, and Marx.

The best of the happy-go-lucky dressers seem to affect sport coats and khaki pants which, on Friday, causes the lobby of our building to look like a scene from "Invasion of the Scoutmasters." Those who aren't in khakis are wearing baggy corduroys that look as though a family of boat people has been living in the seat of their pants. Docksiders, which are the little moccasins held together by leather strings, are the first choice of Friday footwear, but the less stylish are into mutant Hush Puppies.

Among the tacky affectations that have burst upon the Casual Day scene are those dress shirts with no collars, which cause their wearers to look like renegade Quakers. I had always assumed those things were factory seconds.

Lawyers at their leisure are simply not a pretty sight. They tend to be heavily into stretch fabrics and Christmas sweaters. When they shamble through our lobby, I have a powerful urge to accost them and ask, "Are you here for the Doofus Convention?"

The females are more dangerous in terms of casual wear. Some of those fashion victims have reported for work in tank tops and denim revealing heretofore unknown tattoos. ("Born to Dress Bad"?)

Where and when will it all end? What if it spreads to other areas of endeavor? (Picture Ruth Bader Ginsburg forsaking her judicial robes one day a week for a chenille bathrobe. Or undertakers, or worse yet, corpses, dressing down for Friday funerals.)

The only good that I've heard coming out of Casual Day is that young lawyers in some of the firms have been able to hit up tourists for enough spare change to buy lunch. Otherwise, it's "Dress for success—except on Friday." (March 1997)

WOMEN MAY DRESS TO THE NINES, BUT GIVE THEM ZERO FOR FOOTWEAR

There is something afoot in downtown Atlanta that needs some serious looking into and, when I say "afoot," that's just exactly what I mean.

I don't know if the increased radiation in the atmosphere is resulting in some low-level brain damage or if the feminist movement is just manifesting itself in yet another perverse and bizarre fashion protest, but increasing numbers of females have been spotted on the streets of downtown Atlanta dressed to the nines but wearing those grisly running shoes that look like orthopedic possums with laces.

I've always been a fool for high heels but at a tasteful height, of course. I don't favor those ultra-high numbers like Tammie Faye wears on the "PTL Club" that make the wearers look like out of control downhill racers. Nor do I care for those tawdry backless platform jobs that were in vogue a few years back. You know, the ones that seemed to cry out, "Hi, sailor, in town long?"

No, just give me a basic pair of two-inch heels with no gnarled toes poking out the front and I'm quite content and convinced that I. Miller is in his heaven and all is right with the world.

But now, great Ferragamo! Legions of ladies are schlepping up and down Peachtree Street in their secretarial finery or professional female two-piece suits with little Dale Evans string ties, bottomed out with these hideously deformed clodhoppers that look like canvas room-dividers.

Like so many other loathsome trends, this abomination apparently drifted in from New York City. There, at least, it had some meager logical basis in that the working women shod in these Manhattan mutations do, in fact, often walk twenty or thirty blocks to their place of employment. Their Atlanta counterparts generally only have to navigate two or three blocks from the MARTA station nearest their office.

There is a serious lack of logic in this business. Why would these women want to look their worst when they're being seen by the most people they'll be exposed to all day? It causes a flashback in my mind to my teenage years in Bowdon, Georgia, when swarms of our dirt-road debs would come to town on a crowded Saturday afternoon looking like the road show of *The Grapes of Wrath* and wearing so many curlers on their heads that they were picking up Mexican radio stations. All of this just so their hair would look good for some adenoidal adolescent in the back seat of a '52 Chevy at the drive-in movie that night.

This murky business, coupled with a random and unexpected surge of blood to my brain, brought to mind a plethora of vexing questions:

- Why are these women doing this? If their regular shoes are all that uncomfortable, why not wear these canvas club feet all day long and, if comfort is the answer, will they soon start coming to work in their bathrobes?

- What if the male population starts affecting these buffoonish appendages and begins bringing their tassel loafers to work in briefcases?
- Do these pitiful pumps serve some deep unmet need, or will they be just another faddish, female fashion affectation like droopy ballet leg warmers, wearing towels like sarongs at the swimming pool, lip gloss that makes the wearer look like she's just finished off a big glass of Quaker State, grocery shopping in jogging suits, the mandatory sunglasses perched blindly in the top of the head, or, worst of all, those textured hose that look like some exotic leg disease?

I'm sure this too shall pass, but in the meantime, we'll just have to endure yet another fashion fad with all the charm, allure, and sex appeal of an advanced case of athlete's foot. (May 1986)

THE PERILS OF CUSTOM-TAILORED GENES

If current developments continue unchecked, biology may soon be taught as an engineering course.

Accompanying a recent news account there appeared a photo of what looked to be an astronaut dusting a small patch of strawberries with "genetically altered bacteria." While saliva glands on fruit lovers everywhere went into a state of gridlock, the scientists involved giddily proclaimed that the altered bacteria would prevent frost on crops. I would like to think that if whipped cream is not available, most fruit-loving Americans, given a choice between frost and bacteria on their strawberries, would go with frost by at least ten-to-one.

The experiment took place in—where else?—California and was hailed as a major step toward an era in which "advanced tools of molecular biology" would be applied even more widely in agriculture. To hear the scientists involved gloat over the crop-dusting, you would have thought it the biggest breakthrough since George Washington Carver accidentally discovered peanut butter. Haven't these eggheads ever seen *The Little Shop of Horrors*? This stuff could get out of hand…"Little Lamar, eat your vegetables…before they eat you."

My mind's eye flashes toward a tableau at Chez Quiche where some waiter hovering over a table simpers, "Will you take your bacteria over the compote or on the side?"

I was on record against bacteria even before they started genetically altering it. As early as 1980, I publicly urged mandatory testing to root out public officials and athletes suspected of using buttermilk or yogurt.

This tinkering with nature has simply gone too far. Every morning edition brings some new breakthrough in steroid-stuffed chicken, beef or offensive tackles, DNA alterations and high-tech conception. The prestigious *Cobb County Journal of Genetics and Drag-Racing* recently revealed that in 1986 more babies were conceived in laboratories than in drive-in movies. If these science-fiction modes of procreation continue apace, half the population will wind up sending Father's Day cards to some petri dish in Southern California.

Man's preoccupation with improving on nature by scientific means goes back at least as far as Mary Shelley's account of Dr. Frankenstein jump-starting the monster with lightning, and I predict that current attempts with designer genes will have the same unhappy result.

It's not wise to fool Mother Nature. All this talk about altering the DNA so as to root out diseases, rickets, fallen arches, and facial hair represents a dangerous assault on the natural order. People weren't meant to order babies like they buy stereo components—"We'd like the male model 211, with blue eyes, dimples, and hold the cowlick."

What kind of world would it be if everyone looked like Robert Redford? On the other hand, no one would look like Yasser Arafat, so maybe I shouldn't be so quick to criticize. (May 1987)

SALE OF USED ROLEX WATCHES POSES A THREAT TO SOCIETAL ORDER

Call me the Apostle of the Obvious, but I find *The Wall Street Journal* a bit gray and drab (not to be confused with a large Atlanta law firm by the same name). I suspect my impression results in large part by reason of the fact that most of my savings are tied up in a war bond my grandparents gave me in 1943 while the rest are in a bank Christmas Club account that pays no interest.

Beyond that, *The Journal* has no sports section, no funny papers, and no TV listings. However, on a rare and random occasion, it can cough up an interesting kernel or two for the alert reader.

Just last week, as I browsed through an abandoned issue in an airport waiting room, I came across an extraordinary advertisement offering "pre-owned watches, including Rolex, Cartier, Patek-Phillipe [which, until then, I had thought was a French milk of magnesia], etc., at prices starting as low as $400."

The ad featured a beefy-looking pilot in front of a propeller-driven airplane who was described as a "captain with a major American airline." The ad went on to say that Captain Strow (obviously not his real name) "could easily afford a new watch, but he, as thousands before him, opted for the wiser choice... PRE-OWNED!" The ad was placed by Grafstein & Co. ("wholesalers to the Trade since 1939") with establishments in Santa Ana, California, Beverly Hills, and New York.

To illustrate just what bargains were available to wristwatch *arrivistes*, the ad featured a photo of a Rolex SS Gold Datejust that retailed originally for $3,650 but that could be snapped up from Grafstein for a mere $1,790. The ad didn't say what the "SS" stood for, but one assumes "Silly Sap," i.e., one who would pay $3,650 in the first place for a wristwatch that had gold pimples instead of numbers.

It is absolutely mind-boggling (though some have observed that my mind boggles more easily than most) to imagine a business enterprise dealing in used watches that could afford to advertise in *The Wall Street Journal.*

Come with us now through the magic of a sick imagination to the plush Beverly Hills showroom of Grafstein & Co. as some *parvenu* seeks to certify his sociability by upgrading his timepiece:

A salesperson dressed in a pair of pinstriped pants and a black swallow-tailed coat is cooing to the customer, "This particular Rolex was previously owned by a basketball player who turned professional after only three years of college and thus never learned to tell time. I mean, the watch has barely been looked at. It can be yours for a mere $1,790."

Customer (good-naturedly): "What's the 'SS' for? Silly Sap?"

Salesperson (haughtily): "Don't be *jejune*. Besides, that gag was used earlier in the column."

The clear danger (other than a third reference to "SS") is that this trafficking in expensive used watches represents a very dangerous trend. As anyone who has given the matter any serious thought can appreciate, obscenely priced watches have a very important place in our modern society.

Without them, some chump sitting next to an important person would not know that he was a chump and the person next to him was an important person unless the important person was able to flaunt a wristwatch costing roughly as much as a new four-door Hyundai. What then will become of the societal order if every upstart can appear to be an important person simply by buying a Rolex Oyster secondhand?

It's critically important that important people have a clear-cut method of declaring their importance and, while alligator attaché cases, Gucci anythings, and car phones help, nothing else makes such a supercilious statement so succinctly as a stratospherically priced timepiece. (You may wonder at the excessive alliteration in this paragraph. It is intentional. Recent studies by Masters and Johnson have revealed that a significant number of female newspaper readers actually become aroused by a succession of sibilant sounds.)

I don't have any answer for all this, but it's certainly something for you to think about when you're not heavily engaged in other high-minded and challenging activities, like watching "The Newlywed Game" or looking through *The Wall Street Journal* for something interesting to read. (May 1990)

BAN THOSE TV FLIPPERS

A recent study by the National Endowment for the Arts revealed that people are reading less and that those who are still reading are reading thrillers, romances, and science fiction rather than works by "serious" writers, and that adults spend four times more leisure time with the television or radio than with reading materials.

My own private studies have revealed that the average lineman on a college football team has difficulty reading his name on his locker, and even the backs (whose SAT scores, unlike those of the linemen, are often well above room temperature) either move their lips when they read, furrow their brows and use their fingers, or both.

Noted academicians from Yale to the Austell School of Chiropractic and Video Rental are wringing their hands, tearing their hair, and renting their garments. (Another recent study on renting garments revealed that on some college campuses an English professor could rent a tweed sport coat for as much as $3 a day, provided it smelled of pipe smoke and had leather elbow patches.)

While these academic Chicken Littles beat their breasts and cry aloud as to what may be causing this calamitous decline in readership of serious literature, I can pinpoint the reason for it with absolute certainty.

What chance do classics like *Crime and Punishment*, *Remembrance of Things Past*, *Ulysses*, and *The Sass Menagerie* (Longstreet Press, $14.95 in hardback and available at fine bookstores everywhere) have against a sixty-channel cable TV hookup and a remote-control device that permits today's Type-A viewers to do a fly pattern through all channels in under forty-five seconds?

Even widely known intellectuals like myself have been increasingly inclined to eschew worthwhile reading for the ability to watch four movies, the Playboy Channel, and televised meetings of the Atlanta Library Board simultaneously with only the flick of a thumb.

There is, one must concede, an occasional personality so thoroughly torpid that it can withstand the temptation of the almost limitless pleasures offered by remote-control television. If, for example, my wife, by random chance or threat of divorce, should gain control of "the damned flipper," she will sit before the television in a state of narcoleptic rapture and watch the same channel for three or four minutes at a stretch. The woman has absolutely no intellectual curiosity.

I think it goes without saying, however, that even those of us who are beguiled by the wonders offered by remote-control devices would profit from a return to worthwhile reading. What then must be done to staunch the gushing of literary lifeblood now taking place through the precipitous decline in serious readers?

Congress should either

1. ban TV flippers outright
2. require the users to pay a stiff license fee
3. give income tax credits for reading worthwhile literature such as *Moby Dick*, *The Iliad*, *Plutarch's Lives*, and *The Sass Menagerie* (Longstreet Press, $14.95 in hardback and available at fine bookstores everywhere), etc.

Every day the government delays increases the certainty that successive generations of Americans will have the attention span of a water bug and will have body contours approximating a Lazy Boy recliner. Those gentle readers who haven't abandoned this essay in favor of World Federation Wrestling by this point are doubtless asking, "What can I, an average concerned citizen, do about this growing problem?"

Well, you can get your butt out of the Lazy Boy and rush out to invest in some worthwhile literature, such as *The Brothers Karamazov*, *Sartor Resartus*, *Beowulf*, or *The Sass Menagerie* (Longstreet Press, $14.95 in hardback and available at fine bookstores everywhere).

And from this day forth you can let the rallying cry go forward, "We need a whole lot more of Dostoevski and a lot less Danielle Steel!" (November 1989)

YES, IT'S ME AND I'M IN LOVE AGAIN

While drinking in a pre-flight toast the other morning to the unsuspecting client who was funding my first-class air fare to New York, I was stunned to see Ali MacGraw boarding the plane and taking the seat directly behind mine. By sheer coincidence, I had just read an article on Ms. MacGraw in *Interview* magazine the previous weekend and, sensitive soul that I am, was moved to confess to my aging wife that of all the women for whom I would quickly forsake her, Ali MacGraw had long led the list. My wife, unimpressed by my fervent confession, observed that the list had, from time to time, also included Marjorie Main, Minnie Pearl, and the Gish sisters.

Nonetheless, the sight of Ms. MacGraw on Delta 124 in (be still my heart) "the flesh" so fused my mind with concupiscent thoughts that I was, for a fleeting and uncharacteristic moment, speechless.

The sultry Ms. MacGraw, who was accompanied by an aging ex-quarterback named "Frank" or "Fran" Tarklington (or something like that), had been visiting Atlanta in connection with some gala being staged at the sybaritic watering hole, the Limelight.

Her appearance simply defies calm description—eyes as black and shining as soft bituminous coal, skin as smooth and firm as a perfectly ripe casaba melon, and a willowy and taut figure featuring a pair of industrial-strength legs which could easily cause more heart damage than a tank car full of cholesterol. This flawless visage is complemented by the most charming little pearly white front tooth which is endearingly crooked.

Recovering my wits and very, very, casually, I stood up on my seat and turned around to introduce myself. It would be less than honest if I didn't share with you the spark that flashed between us. The quarterback (who must have played for Georgia when they still wore those leather helmets that looked like they should have come with a pair of goggles) was oblivious to Ms. MacGraw's sudden and obvious infatuation with me.

With the legendary dash and verve so characteristic of me, I smoothly engaged her in conversation. We discussed the *Interview* magazine article. We discussed recent books we had both read including *Edie*—I liked it, she liked it, while the quarterback said he was "trying to get through" one of Lewis Grizzard's early works but was having trouble with "all those big words." Finally, yielding to the pleas of the surly stewardess who kept insisting that I prepare for flight, I casually strapped the seatbelt across the back of my legs so as to continue our conversation during takeoff.

At length Ms. MacGraw, clearly unable to deal with her feelings for me, ultimately (and I thought very sweetly) broke off our tête-à-tête by pretending to go to sleep in the middle of one of my sentences. The old quarterback, who still hadn't caught on, was blissfully engrossed in a copy of *Boy's Life*.

While I certainly don't intend to depart from the code of "a gentleman doesn't tell," I think I can reveal something of our relationship by describing the parting scene. While the quarterback gabbed with the gaggle of stewardesses who for some reason kept clustering around him (I think he is on some kind of TV show), Ali (by then we had begun to call each other by our first names) took my hand, looked through my eyes and deep into my soul, and, in a husky voice which, like it or not, revealed her true and secret thoughts, said, "Nice to meet you, Paul." (December 1982)

STATE POLITICIANS DESERVE TO BE FLUSHED WITH VICTORY

With the cost of running election campaigns for state offices now approaching the size of the defense budget or Bill Cosby's take-home pay, it occurred to me during the most recent political hysteria that it is high time to take some drastic measures to reduce the pocketbook pain endured by the candidates and those hapless souls who are called on to fund their interminable and tedious quests for votes.

Voters, quite naturally, become a bit suspicious when candidates who are contending for jobs that pay less than the annual salary of the average Herbal-Life distributor spend multimillions in campaign advertising, all of which looks pretty much alike.

In almost every TV ad the shirt-sleeved candidates appear, oozing sincerity and surrounded by swarms of smiling children, old folks, and minorities. It's mostly the same old crowd telling us how they're going to deliver us from the same old crowd.

Beyond that, scientific research has revealed that prospective voters, after having been bombarded by TV campaign advertisements over a long period of time, become convinced that the candidates are starting to look alike, a dynamic that is somewhat similar to the phenomenon of old married people who begin to resemble each other.

In the interest of improving the electoral process, freeing the airwaves of boring political ads, shortening the political campaigns, and saving the candidates and their public spirited backers literally millions of dollars, I am prepared to advance a modest proposal that involves a new method of political campaigning and voting.

Yes, you heard it here first, the Steed Hydraulic Electoral System.

My system would involve legislation that would prohibit all candidates from soliciting or spending any money for their campaigns. Instead, opposing candidates would get to appear one time on a statewide TV and radio simulcast and in thirty minutes explain why the voters should choose them for high public office.

At the end of the thirty-minute session, a special signal would be given and, at that moment, all voters who favored that particular candidate would race to their bathrooms and flush their toilets. The same procedure would be employed for the next candidate at the end of his harangue.

Water and sewerage systems from Rabun Gap to Tybee Light would then dutifully record the respective pressure drops and report the winners by telephone to the Secretary of State, who could announce the results in minutes. This would also spare us the tedium involved in all those election night TV specials where the regular anchorpersons keep asking Claibourne Darden, "Claibourne, what does all this mean?"

In fact, unless someone was in a great hurry to find out who won, we could even bypass the Secretary of State's declaration and just announce the winners by printing their names on the next month's water bill.

Backwoods voters and those in areas of Cobb County without indoor plumbing would, of course, vote by absentee ballot but, since the Steed Hydraulic Electoral System of voting has a margin of error of ten to fifteen percent, those votes would not be counted as it is unlikely that they would affect the result in any case.

The system is simple, efficient, and reliable and, in my judgment, would have a cathartic effect on voter apathy. Beyond that, it would give new meaning to the term "flushed with victory." (November 1990)

NO FOOL LIKE AN OLD FOOL

There is, they say, no fool like an old fool. (A dispute has ranged for years in philosophical circles as to whom this quote should be attributed, but the authoritative *Barlett's* cites "wives and ex-wives.")

The eternal verity of the maxim is demonstrated regularly as a certain percentage of lawyers my age and older invariably show up for the annual Bar Association Dinner Dance with new mustaches and without old wives and agitate envy in the ranks of their still encumbered colleagues by bringing dates who are but days out of braces and baby fat.

This year's affair was no different, and I had just been helped to the dance floor by my first wife when, bald head glistening, my old friend Matthew appeared at my side wearing a crooked smile and gripping with palsied hand a date who might have had to show her ID to get a drink.

"I'd like for you to meet my date, Tanya," he smirked with obvious pleasure. "Your date?" I said incredulously. "I've got neckties older than this young thing." Ignoring my remark, Matthew, in a voice artificially lowered as a result of sustained concentration at holding in his stomach, began to reel off inane platitudes with the solemn gravity of someone dictating to a stone cutter. All the while, Miss Precious stood by in obvious awe and marveled at these droppings of wisdom.

To spare her, even for a moment, from the certain brain damage I knew would result from overexposure to his mindless ranting, I gallantly asked her to dance. The fact that she was blonde, franticly contoured, and wearing a backless dress with no undershirt doubtless caused some at the gathering to suspect my motives were as much concupiscent as chivalrous.

As we box stepped to the strains of the Bar Association's budget-priced band ("Guy Lumbago and His Three Ruptured Hawaiians"), I assayed her intellect with a few piercing questions.

"Where did you meet Matthew?" I asked as my hand flopped along her bare back like a loose mullet in the bottom of a boat. "At Sanibel, Florida," she cooed. "Well," I smiled suavely, "that's a surprise. Folks his age rarely make it past St. Petersburg. Have you considered the possibility that he may be using you? You know, he may just want you as a donor for his desperately needed hair transplant."

"Oh, I think bald men are so sexy," she squeaked as over her firm, well-rounded shoulder I saw an apparently partnerless Matthew bobbing and jerking about on the dance floor doing what he later characterized as the "Watusi" but which more nearly resembled a poor imitation of Dom DeLuise in the grip of a hernia spasm.

At the end of the evening, as my spouse chauffeured me home (motivated less out of her good nature than a fervent desire to keep the breadwinner out of the County work farm), I speculated aloud, "If someone as bald and unsightly as Matthew can attract a young hardbody like that, just think"—I continued as I smoothed the full, rich, silver hair at my temples (which, it is said, has caused women I barely know to call out my name in their thrashing and troubled slumbers)—"just think what I could get."

"Uh huh," she said dully, "you'd be just like Brother Dave said about the preacher and the money." Before I could ask her to elaborate on her cryptic observation, its full text leaped suddenly and clearly to my mind. She was, in her own inarticulate way, reminding me of a great bit of folk wisdom once uttered by that renowned American philosopher, Brother Dave Gardner, who, when an admirer of his evangelical speaking style suggested he ought to be a preacher "because you could make a million dollars," replied with his legendary maniacal logic, "Dear Heart, what would a preacher *do* with it?"

An experienced wife can crush a fantasy with the flick of her wrist. (May 1983)

KILLING BAMBI: WHY NOT LET THE DEER HAVE GUNS?

We may not be winning the battle against drugs or the battle against crime, but after spending a couple of hours driving on Interstate 20 recently, I am absolutely sure we are winning the battle against Bambi.

My son, son-in-law, and I were returning from a round of golf in Augusta, and in the space of two hours we must have passed at least a hundred vehicles bearing stone-cold deer carcasses. It was very interesting to observe the rolling aftermath of such a monumental slaughter.

All of the hunters affected some sort of "Desert Storm" camouflage outfit, but, in spite of their obvious desire to remain invisible in the woods, most of them also sported orange-colored Day-Glo caps. This might not be as dumb on their part as it would first appear. I suspect it is a psychological gambit that they use to attract the deer. It's easy to imagine a deer saying to his buddy, "Hey Buck, let's go down that trail over there. You won't believe the dork I've spotted in a camouflage suit and orange hat."

All of the hunters were not, as one might imagine, low-browed, hairy-backed males who resembled the characters from the love scene in *Deliverance*. For the most part, except for the paramilitary outfits, they were a pretty ordinary lot, and there were even a few women who apparently joined the carnage on the assumption that "a family that slays together, stays together." (I can just hear the deer-hunter husband now: "Bertha, it gets me so excited to see you field dress a dead buck!")

Their vehicles were big pickup trucks with gun racks in the cab and bumper stickers expressing sentiments such as, "Nuke the Baby Seals." Almost all of them were bearing a glassy-eyed, tongue-protruding dead deer, some containing as many as four.

High-tech mobility has apparently come to the sport, as many of the trucks were carrying four-wheel motor-scooters that are apparently used to track the wily quarry deep into the woods. Some were also carrying little portable seats that, I am told, are somehow placed up in trees to give the hunters yet another advantage in shooting the wary deer. The first advantage, of course, being the fact that the deer themselves are, in most cases, unarmed.

Maybe next year the hunters will outfit their pickups with those huge tires so popular with drivers who have the IQ of mildew and mount a thirty-caliber machine gun on the cab. With this type of rig, they could clearly penetrate even deeper into the woods and substantially increase the body count.

After passing an extraordinary number of these meat wagons, my son-in-law said that one Sunday we ought to rent a pickup and make the same run wearing fake deer heads with one of us lying in the back of the truck in a camouflage suit, glassy-eyed and tongue protruding. For those who might think his suggestion bizarre, I should point out that he once confessed at a public gathering that his all-time favorite movie was *Caddy Shack*.

All of this causes me to wonder what one would do with a dead deer. I know that in some cultures people actually eat them, and I have, in fact, been lured into trying some myself despite fervent protestations that I hate the gamey taste. The standard response is always, "I know, I know, but you haven't tasted it the way I cook it." In fact, I've tasted everything from Deer Stroganoff to Stove-Top Deer Helper and it all tastes like used sandals to me.

There also exists the wonderful possibility that you can chop off the corpse's head, nail it to a board, and hang it on your wall. Almost all schools of interior design agree that there is nothing like a fur-covered deer skull with marbles in its eye sockets to dress up the old recreation room.

All this sounds like I am some sort of animal-rights nut out to ensure that laboratory rats enjoy their full constitutional protections. Actually, I don't have anything at all against the deer hunters or the sport itself. After all, it's a lot closer to nature than grown men dressed in loud-colored sweaters and knickers whacking at a ball with a stick.

However, I have to confess that when I was looking at all those freshly slaughtered deer that day, I did have a flashback of Oscar Wilde's description of fox hunting. He said it was "the unspeakable in full pursuit of the uneatable." (November 1991)

A FEW TIPS FOR STAND-UP COMEDIANS WHO DON'T ALWAYS LEAVE 'EM LAUGHING

Anybody watching television lately has to be aware of the fact that there has been a great comedy explosion. Its hapless victims are sitting around in comedy clubs across the nation with tattered senses of humor and funny things hanging off of their clothes.

There's scarcely a TV cable channel that doesn't feature stand-up comedy these days. (According to noted humor experts, sit-down comedy is in the grip of a severe decline and shows no prospect for a resurgence any time soon.)

Although the comics are, for the most part, entertaining, and a few are funnier than Sam Donaldson's hair, I am perpetually mystified by the fact that when their routine is done, they all, to a man (and sometimes to a woman, in the case of the softer comics), exit abruptly by saying, "You guys have been great. Good night."

This truncated good-bye always leaves me with an empty and unfulfilled sense of *mirthitis interruptus*. One would think that these ultra-clever and hip comedians could come up with something a little more original and humorous when they finally run out of comedy rope.

As a public service, I certified this problem to the prestigious Cobb County Institute of Jocundity and Clever Sayings, an institution devoted to coming up with those hilarious exchanges between TV anchors and their chortling weathermen. They also furnish those side-splitting quips at the end of the articles in *Reader's Digest* and the clever dialogue for fishing shows on cable television. ("All right, son! 'At's a big'un!")

In the space of just two days, their staff, located in small but tastefully decorated offices in the Big Chicken, managed to come up with the following offerings, which I pass along to comics at large as new and improved exit lines:

"My stars, it's nine o'clock (a resourceful comedian will put in the actual time); I've got to go help some friends circumcise their gerbil."

"Well, fun-seekers, I can see by the old comedy dipstick that I've just run out of laughing gas, so, with your permission, I'll just slip off stage and tank up."

"Well, I can tell from the cigarette smoke that it's time for my chest x-ray, so until next time I'll just say *Hawrk! Hawrk! Hawrk!*" (Exit left clutching throat.)

"Well, I can tell from the sea of glassy eyes that you guys can't take even one more hilarious comparison about the difference between living in New York and L.A., so I'm outta here!" (The staff at the Institute points out that comedians, like young waiters and waitresses, refer to everyone as "guys," regardless of gender.)

"*Caramba!* I think my bran flakes are about to kick in, so, like the Cisco Kid's sidekick used to say, 'Let's went.'"

"I'll be leaving now, but I'd like to remind you that a standing ovation would impress the club owner, make me very happy and give all of you a chance to adjust your underwear."

These are just a few examples of snappy closing lines and, until next time, I just want to say, "You guys have been great. Good night." (November 1993)

SEXISTS, PLEASE NOTE: WOMEN'S OBSESSION WITH HAIR MATCHED ONLY BY MEN'S

Ever anxious to avoid even a trace of sexism in my thoughtful and well-reasoned prose, I am careful to root out any suggestion, however subtle, that might be read as supporting the heretical notion that there exist any differences between the male and female of the species.

Notwithstanding this firmly held conviction, my senses will occasionally be jolted by some aberrant fact or circumstance which, by sheer reflex, I'm sure, will cause me to revert to biases I formerly harbored before reaching a state of grace through the assiduous study of the words and works of Alan Alda.

By way of recent example, I was reminded of a prejudice I used to hold to the effect that women seem to have a pathological preoccupation with their hair that is not shared with the same unwholesome fervor by males.

This dangerous flashback was occasioned when I read a human-interest story in the morning paper about an elderly Atlanta legal secretary who had retired to Roopville, Georgia, and was living with two cats in a disabled '73 Pontiac so that her thirty-seven dogs could enjoy her house trailer. Neighbors, concerned by indications that the lady was severely neglecting her four-legged friends, had called in the appropriate authorities to assess the situation.

The investigators discovered that she had indeed sacrificed her quarters, her Social Security checks, and all manner of personal comforts and necessities so that this Malthusian mob of mutts would be comfortably sustained.

Happily, an "animal welfare group" interested in the upkeep of stray dogs was located and cash was promised to ameliorate the woman's plight. This is where my flashback flashed. After saying that the extra money would permit her to feed and fence her dogs and reclaim her quarters, she concluded with this amazing statement: "And I'd like to do something about my hair."

It gives one pause that a woman who has chosen a life of self-sacrifice so extreme as to live in the hulk of a busted Pontiac would still, at the prospect of sunnier times, think about her long-neglected coif.

I had long observed that the mood of my sinewy spouse was adversely affected with every change in the length or hue of her hair, which, at one unhappy point, was switching colors with the frequency of a chameleon scurrying around a Christmas tree. I also recalled that when I pressed my oldest daughter, Georgia, to consider Tulane as a college that she might seek to attend, she summarily dismissed the idea by saying, "Are you kidding? That humidity in New Orleans would make my hair fall."

The unhealthy and sexist thought became so strong that I could only overcome it by watching some videotapes of old Phil Donahue shows, and, I'm happy to report, reason finally began to regain control.

And the reasoned answer is that both women and men are equally obsessive about their hair, and you need to go no farther than your nearest TV to verify this fact. John Forsyth of *Dynasty* fame has gone to a rinse so purple that his head looks like a grape with a part in it. Jim Bakker of the "PTL Club" turned silky blond overnight in a miracle more likely wrought by Miss Clairol than divine intervention. Evangelist Ernest Angley, not trusting his own formidable healing powers to restore his missing hair, appears to have covered his noggin with a toupee that looks like a piece of Astroturf.

It was a great relief to be back in harmony with the mainstream of modern feminist thought. As an interesting aside, I might point out that my uncle, George Lee Steed, was one of Roopville's most innovative mayors. He fulfilled a campaign promise to double the city's revenue by simply installing a second parking meter.

Later, as a solution to Roopville's traffic congestion, he ordered that all streets be made one-way. Over three-fourths of the community found themselves stranded in nearby Franklin, Georgia, before it was discovered that Roopville had only one street.

The former mayor could not be reached for comment about the story involving the lady and her dogs. (October 1985)

THERE'S SOMETHING FISHY ABOUT THOSE SUSHI BARS

On a recent trip to Los Angeles, a lawyer friend of mine there offered to take me to dinner at a sushi bar and I eagerly accepted. I assumed we were going to one of those Japanese restaurants that is a combination between a catfish house and the old *Ed Sullivan Show*, where wiry waiters juggle kitchen utensils, shrimps, and condiments and stage periodic grease fires on a communal griddle.

I enjoy those outings in that the theater is entertaining and the food, if not cooked sufficiently for one's liking, can be slipped surreptitiously back on the griddle at the end of a chopstick and rendered edible in time. I have always belonged to the school of gastronomic thought that if something couldn't be battered, fried, and chewed, it was not a legitimate foodstuff. In the outlawed category would fall such titans of queasiness as raw oysters, boiled okra, and that darling of bridge clubs and family reunions alike, aspic.

Like a lamb entering an abattoir, I was led by my friend into a small Japanese eatery as antiseptic in appearance as the inside of a Frigidaire. Everything was black, white, and lacquered, and the menu, which featured esoteric entrees such as "maguro, toro, hamachi and saba," offered no clue of the quivering and slithery selections that were soon to be placed right under our noses.

Noting my rising state of befuddlement, my companion airily offered to order for both of us and muttered a series of oriental incantations to the eager and beaming waiter.

I should have been suspicious at the outset, as California is widely known as an incubator for every form of weird comestible ranging from tofu, frozen yogurt, and bean sprouts to trail mix and granola. In fact, some savants have suggested that granola is itself an appropriate metaphor for California in that "everything that ain't fruits or flakes is nuts." However, I was simply not prepared for the platter of colorful, slippery delicacies that was placed before me.

It turns out that sushi consists exclusively of uncooked fish and fish by-products arranged in colorful little balls or geometric patterns. Of course it's colorful—the stuff hasn't been near a stove. Suppressing an involuntary shiver, I said to my companion, "I hate to be a chicken of the sea, but I'm not eating any of that stuff. If God wanted us to eat raw fish, He would have given us nine lives."

"Oh," she said, "you really ought to try the tobiko; it's flying fish roe, and the bright orange eggs are firm and salty and almost explode with flavor when you bite them."

"Not in this lifetime, Jacques Cousteau breath," I gagged. "Maybe if Mr. Moto over there could zap these beauties in the microwave I'd be willing to give them a nibble around the edges."

Rolling her eyes to convey her dismay at being with such a culinary yahoo, my friend dived into the briny offerings with the gusto of a bear catching salmon in the Columbia River while I sought to stave off hunger pangs with a pack of stale Rolaids.

It is a staggering notion to think that there are grown people out there paying $19.95 for a mess of codfish colons artfully arranged to look like a platter of sweetheart roses. I have formed a committee of concerned citizens to press for legislation requiring warning labels on sushi bar menus reading something like, "The Surgeon General has determined that gobbling uncooked marine offal will cause permanent damage to your gag reflex and may turn your liver into a doorstop."

While California is obviously the hotbed of this kamikaze cuisine (there is even a combination French and sushi restaurant on Rodeo Drive called "Chez Hepatitis"), evidence exists that the trend is spreading. I have overheard yuppies in downtown elevators rapturously extolling the virtues of squid spleens and carp chitterling to one another and even heard that the fishy fad had reached Cobb County. However, I checked out the Cobb County rumor and it turned out to be a false alarm. It seems that the deep fat fryer at the Rio Vista in Marietta was on the blink and some of the catfish came out undercooked.

However, to demonstrate just how widespread the threat has become, I learned from a friend in Birmingham that sushi had even spread to darkest Alabama. "The only difference," he said, "is that in Alabama we call it 'bait.'"

Kelp! (September 1987)